On Wings of Fortune

ON WINGS OF FORTUNE
A BOMBER PILOT'S WAR

from THE BATTLE OF BRITAIN,
to THE AIR OFFENSIVE AGAINST GERMANY,
BOMBING *in* NORTH AFRICA *and*
Accident Investigation in THE FAR EAST

WING COMMANDER RICHARD PINKHAM
DFC (RAF RET.)
with STEVE DARLOW

Published in 2010 by Fighting High Ltd,
23 Hitchin Road, Stotfold, Hitchin, Herts, SG5 4HP
www.fightinghigh.com

British Library Cataloguing-in-Publication data.
A CIP record for this title is available from the
British Library.

ISBN – 13: 9780956269621

Designed and typeset in Monotype Baskerville
11/14pt and Monotype Akzidenz Grotesk 10/14pt
by Michael Lindley www.truthstudio.co.uk

Printed and bound by Toppan Printing Co. (UK) Ltd.

Contents

Introduction *by Steve Darlow*

It was really by chance that I came across Richard Pinkham's manuscript. I had made contact with Richard, via the No. 77 Squadron Association, to ask permission to quote a few of his experiences in my book *Special Op Bomber*, and volume 1 of the Fighting High series. When I met Richard he asked if I would be interested in having a look at a book he had written based on the diaries he kept during the war. As soon as I started reading, it became clear that this was a valuable memoir recording the experiences of a Bomber Command airman who flew in the early days of the air offensive. In addition, Richard's account went on to describe his fascinating role in accident investigation in the Far East – a subject matter that has rarely been touched on. Very soon there was no doubt in my mind that Richard's story should be published.

When we were planning the book, Richard's wife had suggested the title 'As Luck Would Have It!' Richard was keen, as he considered luck had been a significant contributor to his survival. Most surviving Bomber Command airmen accept that luck was a factor throughout their operational careers. There was always the risk of collision over a target, or of bombs falling from above onto your aircraft. It could be that your aircraft was on the wrong side of the probability statistic calculations in a flak barrage, or was the one that was latched onto by searchlight beams. The serviceability of flying instruments could be unpredictable, and then there were the vagaries of the weather over Europe and the United Kingdom – cloud, high winds and storms, apart from the risk of ice clasping your aircraft and forcing a struggle with aerodynamics and gravity. Or you could return from a long flight and find your airfield enshrouded in fog, leaving you to try desperately to find somewhere to land with your last drops of fuel.

Luck indeed was a factor in survival, and the airmen could never completely eradicate risk and exposure to the fortunes of war. Many fine pilots and experienced crews were lost in unfortunate incidents and unlucky circumstances. But airmen could offset the risks with flying skill, bomber-crew teamwork and efficiency, and experience.

And so, with regard to the title of this book, Richard and I settled on the title *On Wings of Fortune*. Richard was fortunate to have survived and he has no hesitation in accepting that. A statistical analysis of the attrition on raids that Richard took part in (see Appendix 3) shows that he had a 1 in 5 chance of surviving. Richard did survive and was able to go on and tell his story; 55,500 of his Bomber Command colleagues could not do the same.

With regard to the structure of this book, Richard takes us through his entire operational flying career, providing details of all his sorties against the enemy. In addition, we are treated to anecdotes – humorous, interesting and tragic – from his experiences away from the front-line squadrons. I was keen to provide the reader with the context of Richard's experiences, but, rather than break up the flow of Richard's narrative, I have added inserts to describe the nature of the operations and also to add some detail.

As someone who has spent over a decade researching the bomber offensive I found Richard's story particularly interesting in that it provides an insight into the early days of the Royal Air Force bomber war, when much of the flying and bomb aiming was by dead reckoning. The aerial battles of attrition fought by Bomber Command in the second half of the war have been written about extensively, but the exploits of the pioneers of the bomber offensive have filled fewer pages. Richard completed two tours of operations on bombers. His first, with No. 77 Squadron, carried out when his country was directly under attack from the Luftwaffe and under the threat of a seaborne (and possibly airborne) invasion, provides the 'view from the cockpit' as he flew in defence of the United Kingdom and also took the offensive back to Germany. Compared to the size and intensity of later bomber raids on Germany, these early attacks would appear to be mere pinpricks, yet they were a necessary step in the process. And the morale impact of these sorties must not be overlooked. The British population's spirit was bolstered in the knowledge that the Royal Air Force could hit back and Germany's High Command was made fully aware that their cities were within range. Resources, in growing numbers, would have to be channelled into the defence of the Third Reich, away from any other war-making programmes.

Richard's second tour in 1942, with No. 150 Squadron, took place at a time when the night air battle over Germany was escalating, as reflected in his personal experiences. The attrition rates were high. Richard then transferred with the squadron to North Africa to take part in the expulsion of the Axis forces from Tunisia. Finally, we travel with Richard to India and Burma, where he was tasked with investigating the cause of air accidents, work that often involved trips deep into the jungle, and for which he was provided with his own personal Spitfire!

At the time of compiling this book Richard was in his ninety-third year, and preparations were under-way in the aviation heritage fraternity to celebrate the seventieth anniversary of the Battle of Britain. The activities of the fighter boys of 1940 must, of course, be celebrated, but the truly unsung heroes of 1940, the bomber boys who were fighting back, must also be recognised. Richard Pinkham was one of those other 'Few', and it has been my privilege to work with him on this book and to publish the exploits of a Bomber Command hero.

Prologue

2 July 1940
No. 77 Squadron
RAF Driffield, Yorkshire, England.

Briefing was scheduled for 1400 hours. The briefing room was bright and spacious, and folding wooden tables were set out in rows, at which were seated aircrews of both squadrons – in all about 150 officers and NCO pilots, navigators, wireless operators and air gunners. There was a general buzz of subdued conversation, mainly speculating on the probability of the target.

On the wall, facing the assembly, was displayed a large map of Europe. A red tape, pinned to the map, extended from a location in Yorkshire, near the coast, to another point north-east of Brussels. The tape formed a dog-leg at Spurn Head at the mouth of the Humber River. From there it deviated slightly to a point on the island of Walcheren on the Dutch coast.

On the dot at 1400 hours, the Duty Operations Officer called the assembled crews to attention as the Station Commander, followed by both Squadron Commanding Officers, entered. There was complete silence, and the atmosphere was filled with tense expectation. 'At ease,' intoned the Station Commander, and everyone took to their seats again. He made a short introduction announcing the target for tonight; it was the Evere airport at Brussels. The Duty Operations Officer then took the stage, and target maps were distributed to every captain. Crew members huddled round their captain studying details carefully, noting in particular the red type at the top: 'HOSPITALS ARE MARKED + AND MUST BE AVOIDED.' We also noted that there were three such red crosses in Brussels itself but that the target was 3 miles to the north-east of the city centre [see Appendix 2]. Only the most clueless could possibly drop bombs anywhere near the hospitals. The Operations

Officer explained that the object was to put the airfield out of action, so as to deny its use to fighter squadrons based there. A large wall map was revealed and the route marked in red tape. We were told that the route took us well away from defended areas, and that flak over the target area had been reported as 'slight'. The Met Officer then gave details of the weather forecast. There would be very little cloud, both en route and over the target area.

I felt my heartbeat quicken slightly, as I realised 'this is it'. For me, this was the culmination of less than ten months' training. From my first dual flight on a Miles Magister, I was to be flying my first operational sortie.

1. Nothing Else but Flying

Richard Mansfield Pinkham was born on 18 June 1916, and lived with his family in Witham, Essex. He was the son and grandson of the owners of the company firm Pinkham Gloves. Richard was educated at Colchester Royal Grammar School but did not sit for matriculation. His father thought he would learn more in the family business, and Richard left school at 17. But at that stage of his life he was simply not motivated for business. Something else had fired his imagination. Once, while on holiday in Great Yarmouth, he had been given the opportunity to take a short flight in a bi-plane. There was no looking back.

No. 19 E&R FTS, Gatwick and Fairoaks

From earliest boyhood, I had dreamed of nothing else but flying. I had only one ambition: this burning desire to fly. My father, however, had other ideas for me. He wanted me to follow in the family business. But my heart was not in it, and we were constantly having rows. The opportunity I was waiting for came when the Royal Air Force launched a campaign to recruit pilots to serve on a short service commission, and I applied. I was notified to attend an interview at the Air Ministry, much to my father's disapproval and disdain.

I do not think I impressed the selection board when it came to the question of my scholastic achievements. Had I matriculated in any subject?

'No. I left school before sitting for "matric".'

'In what subjects did you pass?'

'French and Art,' I replied meekly.

'That's not particularly brilliant!'

The way the interview was going I felt sure there was no hope of me being selected. So I thought there was nothing to lose.

'Do you have to be particularly brilliant to get a commission?' I retorted.

I had already passed the medical examination, with flying colours, but, of some forty applicants on this draft, only two had passed the full medical, so it appeared that there was a desperate need for pilots. Those who failed the medical standard for pilots were selected for training as navigators, wireless operators, gunners and bomb aimers.

In due course I was notified to report to Gatwick for initial training. I first met the chaps with whom I was to spend the next few months training when we assembled on the platform at Redhill, to change for the train to Gatwick. Most of them were not much older than sixth-form boys; few were more than 24 years old. We arrived at Gatwick station, where we were joined by another group, which brought the total up to about forty.

The old Gatwick aerodrome building was a large two-storey circular building with the aerodrome control placed on top in the middle. A concrete apron and taxi tracks covered the ground in front of the building, on which were parked a number of Magister trainer aircraft. We were conducted to the main hall in the airport building, quickly kitted out with Sidcot flying overalls, and introduced to our respective instructors. There were thirty-seven 'pupil' pilots, as we were called, and one instructor to every two pupils. My instructor lost no time in taking me out to a Magister aircraft, parked neatly alongside a dozen or so similar aeroplanes. After a very quick instruction on the essential controls, a safety check round the aircraft, and verification that I was properly strapped in, we set off to the take-off point. We were given permission to take off from the control pilot, and flew around for twenty-five minutes, as recorded in my logbook, for 'effect of controls and air experience' (8 August 1939).

My instructor was a very patient man. He needed to be. I do not know how he got on with the other pupil pilots, but he certainly had his patience sorely tested with me. Most trainee pilots were to be allowed to go solo after five hours of dual instruction. After eight hours' dual instruction, I was still not considered by my instructor to be 'safe' to go solo. However, out of sheer frustration he said, 'This time you are on your own, and break your own neck if you want to! You are not going to break mine. You are not really concentrating hard enough. Unless I see the sweat pouring off your face, I shall not believe you are really trying.' This was one of the hottest days that summer, and I thought, 'God. In this heat and flying kit, how much hotter do I have to get?' 'You are on your own,' he said. The sweat started to run down my face as I realised this was it: s**t or bust! It had a wonderful effect of concentrating the mind.

This was the moment I had waited for, the realisation of years of boyhood dreams. The truth of it was that I had imagined that flying was going to be easy! It was subsequently drummed into me that probably the worst sin for a pilot was overconfidence; the antidote was concentration.

My instructor was left standing on the airfield as I taxied over to the take-off point, carried out the cockpit check and turned the aircraft across wind, at the same time casting an eye over my right shoulder. No other aircraft was in the circuit. As soon as I received a green light from the aerodrome control pilot, I turned the aircraft into the wind. 'God,' I thought, 'this is it!' I completed the circuit, everything went according to the manual, and coming in to land I eased the stick back and the 'Maggie' (Magister) touched down like a feather! I could hardly believe my luck, and neither could the instructor. I taxied back to where I had left him standing. 'Beginner's luck!' he said cynically. 'Go round and do it again.' Needless to say, I was full of self-confidence by then, and of course the next landing gave a good imitation of a rabbit. I held off about 3 feet too high, and the aircraft bounced heavily. Fortunately these aircraft were designed to take such punishment.

Over in the corner of the airfield were two large hangars, which were out of bounds to all but the trusted few who were working inside. There were rumours that inside was Britain's answer to Hitler's secret weapon. For some of us aspiring Aces, overwhelmed with curiosity, the opportunity presented itself for us to take a closer look at the mysteries inside when the hangar doors were left slightly ajar. We sauntered casually in close vicinity of the hangar, and our curiosity was even more aroused when we beheld what in those days were enormous gleaming silver bombers. Being still uninitiated in aircraft identification, we could only stand in awe. Little did we realise then that, in the not too distant future, some of us would be posted to an Operational Training Unit (OTU) to receive training as bomber pilots and would become competent to fly them. The thought of ever being capable of flying one of those monsters seemed a very remote dream.

It was a glorious sunny morning, on that fateful day in September 1939, that found a group of young and desperately keen budding Air Aces

listening solemnly to Neville Chamberlain announcing those fateful
words: 'I have received no such undertaking.' It brought home the reality
of the situation: that among us there were those who were in fact
destined to become real Air Aces.

Some of us were already wearing Sidcot flying suits, standing by
awaiting a turn to go up to do some circuits and bumps; others were still
in civvies, about to go to a classroom for a lecture on air navigation,
airframes, or some other aspect of elementary flying training. This was
in fact No. 19 Elementary Flying Training School. It seemed a most
unlikely place; there were no runways, no massive terminal buildings, no
vast car parks, just a very small airport building and control tower, and
the two large hangars, out of the way on the edge of the airfield.

We were assembled in the airport lounge in stunned silence as
Mr Chamberlain announced that we were at war. No one quite knew
what to do next. There was no cheering, but we were shaken out of our
mesmerised shock, as wailing sirens broke the spell. At the sound of the
sirens we fully expected the sky to be darkened with hundreds of
German bombers. We made a dash to the nearest slit trenches, which
were located on the periphery of the airfield, a distance of about
200 yards. We covered the distance in what was probably an Olympic
world record. The sight of all those fellows sprinting in full flying gear
put one in mind of a Sports Day fancy dress race. The impression was
rather of frightened rabbits scurrying for shelter in their burrows at the
first sound of gunshot. The analogy was complete when, shortly after,
the 'all clear' was sounded, and, one by one, heads started to emerge
above the slit trenches. No bombers appeared, so everyone got back to
learning about flying and how to fly.

After a month at Gatwick the course was transferred to Fairoaks airfield,
where we completed an Elementary Flying Training course on Tiger
Moths. The time passed quickly and uneventfully. The day came when
we were assembled to hear what fate had in store for us. It was a sort of
separating of the sheep from the goats: those who were to be sent to
advanced training on single-engine aircraft, which meant fighters or
fighter-bombers; and the rest, who were to be sent to training on twin-
engines. We imagined that all the best pilots would be selected for
fighters and those who remained would be unfortunate enough to go on
to bombers.

Names were read out. Those selected to go on to Hawker Harts were thought to be 'Lucky Sods!' The rest, myself included, would be going on to Airspeed Oxfords. There was disappointment for many who were not selected for fighters, as they had aspired to be Aces. Eventually those selected for 'twins' had every reason to be thankful that they had not gone on to fighter squadrons, as the losses were terrible. At least those selected for advanced training were happy that they had not been thrown out, as some were who had just not made the grade.

Another month passed quickly on Tiger Moths at Fairoaks, and then we were all posted to Hastings for 'disciplinary' training. This involved drill and PT on the sea front, in an attempt to put a bit of backbone into us, to instil the rudiments of discipline, and to make men of us. It was late October and the weather was seasonal for the time of the year, with strong winds and cold temperatures. The PT instructor was a typically sadistic type. One morning, after about an hour of really strenuous PT, he gave the order: 'Every man into the sea and the last man in is a cissy.' It was cold enough to freeze the proverbial brass monkey.

But, despite the rigours of square bashing, the fortnight at Hastings had its pleasurable moments. In fact, I could say that the fortnight in Hastings had some very pleasurable moments. My brother, who had not joined up, was under-manager at the Queens Hotel at the time. We had not seen each other for some time, and needless to say I paid him a surprise visit as soon as I arrived. We had a good old natter, catching up on family news. I spent most evenings with him in the bar at his hotel, and he introduced me to a number of his friends. One who appealed to me in particular was Pat. She was breathtakingly beautiful, with long blonde hair and an exquisite figure. I took her to the theatre to see *When We Are Married*. After that we spent every evening together.

No. 3 SFTS, South Cerney

I had been writing to a girl I had met in Manchester a few years earlier, called Marie. We corresponded from time to time, but it was on a purely platonic basis. When she learned I had joined the Royal Air Force, she wrote saying that she would love to see me again.

Although I had known Pat for only a short while, we had become very fond of each other. We spent the whole of my last day at Hastings together. On Sunday, 22 October, our course detachment set off by train for South Cerney in Gloucestershire. We were not sorry to leave Hastings, as it could hardly have been described as a holiday resort while we were there. For me it had been made tolerable by meeting Pat and spending all my spare time with her. We said goodbye and we agreed to keep in touch. As I had no idea where I would be likely to get posted, we made no plan to meet, but she said she would try to get up to see me at Cirencester. I did not take too much notice of that, as I did not think she cared that much for me. So, as I had not taken her intention too seriously, I was more than surprised when she phoned me at South Cerney, after I had been there only a month, to say that she would like to come and spend a week with me, and would I book accommodation for her at the Golden Fleece. She spent the whole of the last week of November with me. Although we had developed a strong attraction for each other, I did not feel I was in love with her. After spending a wonderful week together we said goodbye, but we did not arrange to meet again.

In the meantime I had received two or three letters from Marie and had already formed a strong impression that she was something exceptional. Her letters were very caring, understanding, warm-hearted and sincere. I had fourteen days' leave for Christmas, so she invited me to meet her parents at Birkdale and to spend Christmas with her and her family. By the end of my leave I had fallen head over heels in love with her. She was so full of life, and vivacious, with such a warm personality. I decided she was the one I wanted to marry. She was completely different from Pat. She was petite, energetic, spirited, warm, gentle and affectionate. She had vivid blue eyes, dark soft fine hair and a smile that radiated sunshine. Although Pat was a very attractive girl, I suppose it was making the comparison between the two girls that helped me decide. We met a couple of times again whenever I had a spot of leave, and on 19 March we became engaged.

After four months' training on Oxfords we completed the course on 26 April 1940. We were awarded our Wings and I was passed out as a 'good average pilot'. The following day my father was getting married, my mother having died some four years before. So it was quite fortuitous that, as I had some leave, I was able to join in the marriage ceremony. I had arranged to meet Marie the night before in London, and we would spend the night at a hotel. I arranged to meet her at Paddington. I had to make the connection with the train for Paddington at Swindon and phone Marie to meet me at Paddington Terminus. I got to Swindon with little time to spare, but in the blackout I got on the wrong platform. The train I caught was going to Bath! When I got to Bath I contacted the station master and asked him to have a notice displayed at Paddington, to the effect that I would be three hours late meeting Marie. I got the train from Bath, and sure enough, when I arrived at Paddington, Marie was there waiting for me. I thought any girl who would wait three hours for me must be worth marrying.

Early in May 1940 I was posted to No. 10 Operational Training Unit at Abingdon for training on Armstrong Whitworth Whitley aircraft. I received my first dual instruction on 22 May and was detailed to fly my first and only solo night cross-country one month later, before being posted to an operational squadron the following day.

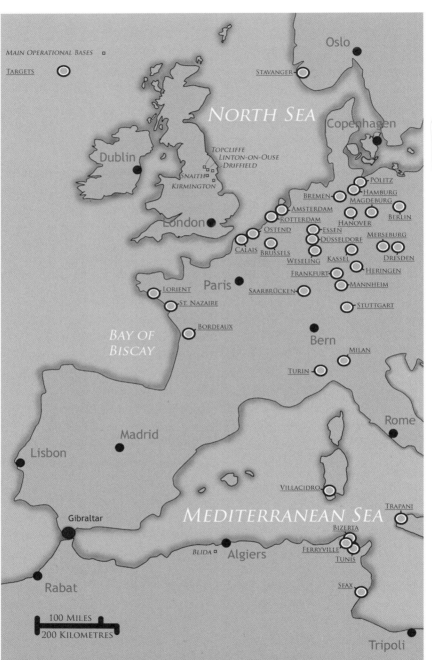

MAIN OPERATIONAL BASES □
TARGETS ◎

Oslo

STAVANGER

NORTH SEA

Copenhagen

Dublin

TOPCLIFFE
LINTON-ON-OUSE
DRIFFIELD
SNAITH
KIRMINGTON

POLITZ
BREMEN
HAMBURG
MAGDEBURG
AMSTERDAM
BERLIN
ROTTERDAM
HANOVER
London
OSTEND
ESSEN
MERSEBURG
CALAIS
DÜSSELDORF
DRESDEN
BRUSSELS
KASSEL
WESELING
Paris
FRANKFURT
HERINGEN
LORIENT
SAARBRÜCKEN
MANNHEIM
ST. NAZAIRE
STUTTGART

BAY OF
BISCAY
BORDEAUX

Bern

MILAN
TURIN

Rome

Madrid

Lisbon

VILLACIDRO

TRAPANI

Gibraltar

MEDITERRANEAN SEA

BIZERTA
BLIDA □
Algiers
FERRYVILLE
TUNIS

Rabat

SFAX

100 MILES
200 KILOMETRES

Tripoli

RICHARD PINKHAM'S TOUR OF OPERATIONS
OPERATIONAL TARGETS AND MAIN OPERATIONAL BASES

2. War and Reality

During the 1930s, with another war against Germany shifting further from a possibility to a probability, Britain set about rearming. Aerial bombardment was seen as playing a much larger role in a future conflict than had been the case in the First World War, and the British government set about reallocating defence funds to give a much greater share to the expansion of the Royal Air Force. Plans were put in place to construct new airfields, 'modern' bombers were designed and took to the air, and recruitment initiatives attracted young men to the thrill of being able to fly. In 1936 Bomber Command was formed, along with Fighter Command, Coastal Command and Training Command.

When all hopes of peace finally evaporated following the German invasion of Poland, Britain declared war on the aggressor in September 1939. The RAF's Bomber Command was in no position to play a short-term war-winning role. The battle front lay hundreds of miles away. A force of 280 aircraft filled 23 front-line squadrons, and the airmen were restricted in that they were ordered to ensure that no civilian areas were hit; coastal targets became a priority. In addition, some of Bomber Command's strength had been siphoned off for operations with the Advance Air Striking Force in France.

So the UK-based Royal Air Force Bomber Command could do little in the first few months of the war to influence the battles in the East substantially, but operations were flown and lessons were learned, notably that daylight operations were going to be costly. While Norway and Denmark fell to the Germans in April 1940, Bomber Command's daylight attempts to attack enemy shipping proved high-priced, as historians Martin Middlebrook and Chris Everitt record in *The Bomber Command War Diaries*:

> Bomber Command entered into its Norway operations with enthusiasm but almost immediately suffered a setback when nine Hampdens and

Wellingtons were shot down, most of them by German fighters, in a daylight raid on shipping in the Stavanger area. These losses finally convinced Bomber Command that the self-defending daylight bomber formation theory was not valid and this day, 12 April 1940, marked the end of the pre-war bombing policy; it was undoubtedly the most important turning-point in Bomber Command's war.[1]

During the Blitzkrieg of May and June 1940, as France, Belgium and Holland fell, there was another significant turning-point when the Germans bombed Rotterdam on 15 May 1940. Restrictions on British bomber crews not to cross the river Rhine were lifted and RAF bomber pilots, that very night, took their explosives to industrial targets in Hitler's Reich. In June 1940 German commanders were in a position where they could stand and view their enemy's coastline across the English Channel and contemplate an invasion of their mauled opponent. The Battle of Britain, a battle of survival, was about to start. The fighter pilots of the RAF would be called upon to defend British skies, the bomber crews would be called upon to fight back and prove that the RAF was not defeated and could oppose an invasion and inflict their own wounds on the enemy. It was a desperate time; it truly was about the survival of Britain and everything depended upon the ability of the RAF in this fight for existence. Much depended on the 'Few' in their Spitfires and Hurricanes. Much also depended on the 'other Few', the bomber boys, men like Richard Pinkham in their Battles, Blenheims, Hampdens, Whitleys and Wellingtons.

No. 77 Squadron, RAF Driffield

It was already quite light on the morning of 30 June 1940 when I arrived at Driffield at 0700 hours, to take up operational duties with No. 77 Squadron, having travelled from Abingdon through the night. I viewed RAF Driffield through rather bleary eyes. This then was the real thing. My heart was beating like a drum with the excitement of the prospect of what was to come. But nothing that my wildest imagination could conceive of was as dramatic as what turned out to be the reality.

The night before Richard arrived at Driffield, Whitleys of No. 77 Squadron had been taking part in an attack on the Hochst Explosives Factory in Frankfurt. Bomber Command had sent eighty-three aircraft to various targets, three of which would not return; one flown by No. 77 Squadron's Squadron Leader Mark Hastings with no survivors from the crew of five.[2]

There was already an air of urgency as I 'booked in' and reported to the station adjutant. I was conducted to the Officers' Mess, where I dumped my kit, had a quick wash and brush-up, and got some breakfast. I reported back to the Adjutant, who in turn took me to be introduced to the commanding officer, Wing Commander Jarman. Although this was an awesome experience, I could see immediately that this was a man who commanded respect and was one to be admired. Later I was introduced to my flight commander of 'A' flight, Squadron Leader Howard, a no-nonsense type of fellow, with a quiet disposition and a very upright bearing. He remained with the squadron until the end of January 1941.

My initial impression of urgency was well founded. As soon as I had been allocated a locker, I was detailed to fly a Magister to ferry a pilot to Mamby to collect a Wimpey (Wellington) for the squadron, and return – a round trip that took two hours twenty minutes. As soon as I returned, I was informed that I was to do a night cross-country with my new skipper, Pilot Officer North. My only previous experience of a night cross-country had been on the very last night at No. 10 OTU, before I was posted to Driffield. Fortunately it was the policy for new pilots to fly as a 'second dickie' on ops, to gain experience before being made a captain.

The following night we were detailed to carry out an attack on the airfield at Brussels on the outskirts of the city, a quick in and out. The trip took just over three hours to get there, so there was no need to have overload fuel tanks fitted. Consequently there was more room for bombs. We carried the maximum bomb load, a total of four 500lb and six 250lb bombs, which were carried in the wings.

No. 77 Squadron sent ten Whitley Vs to bomb the airfield on the night of 2–3 July 1940, including Whitley N1501, flown by Pilot Officer North, with co-pilot Pilot Officer Pinkham, and crew of Sergeant Savill, Sergeant Briggs and Sergeant Croome. Time up 2205 hours. Time down 0420 hours.

The whole trip was a piece of cake. Flying at 12,000 feet, we were well above the range of light flak, and the heavy flak did not bother us. As I was second dickie, all I could do was to stand to one side, beside the pilot, and take in all that I could see. This was my first experience of anti-aircraft fire, and I was quite fascinated to watch the tracer shells coming towards us, apparently very slowly, looking like a string of pearls, arcing as they reached the limit of their range and moving much faster. Black puffs of smoke appeared all round us, as the heavy ack-ack shells burst, but well away from us, so they did not present any real danger. There was a sense of surrealism about it, but any element of possible danger just did not occur to me. Then very bright lights started appearing, as other aircraft around the target dropped their parachute flares to illuminate the target for a clear view for the bomb-aimer. These were followed by brilliant dazzling flashes, as aircraft dropped photo-flashes, which were synchronised with the bombs being dropped, to take a photograph of the target.

We approached the target, and the bomb-aimer, already in his prone position, peered into the darkness, endeavouring to pick out a good pin-point from which he could give the skipper directions to the target. He called for a flare to be released. The wireless operator, who had been keeping a listening watch, left his set to go back to release the flare. The flare burst, casting a brilliant light over the whole area, providing the bomb-aimer with a good view of the target. He was then virtually in control of the aircraft, giving the pilot directions right up to the point when he pressed the bomb release.

The bomb-aimer called out, 'Open bomb doors.'

'Bomb doors open,' responded the skipper.

'More to port skipper.'

The voice of the bomb-aimer came through the intercom. Seconds passed, which would seem like hours, as we waited for the bomb-aimer to call again.

'OK skipper, left a bit – steady – left – left, steady – right a bit – steady – steady – hold it – steady.'

Then a pause of several seconds before 'Bombs gone'. We knew the bombs had gone, as we felt the kite lift as it was relieved of its load.

'Let's get the hell out of here,' called the skipper.

'Can you see anything Nick?' the skipper asked the rear gunner, who generally had a good view of the bombs bursting below us.

'Not yet skipper.' Then, 'There they go! Wow! I can't see if we've hit anything, it's too dark.' A pause then, 'Yes, we've hit something – there's a bloody big explosion and fire but I can't see what it is.'

'Johnny,' the skipper called to the navigator, 'give me a course for home.

'Three O five degrees, skipper – ETA coast 25 minutes.'

Skipper set his compass on the heading given him by the navigator

and, banking gradually to port, brought the aircraft round onto the
heading for the Dutch coast. Each member of the crew settled down to
his respective tasks for the run home. We were well clear of the flak
defences, and the course given by the navigator would keep us well clear
of any defences until we passed the coast. No one spoke. Each member
of the crew was preoccupied with his own thoughts, each one relieved
that they had escaped unscathed. The return flight was uneventful. We
crossed the Dutch coast dead on track, and altered course for Spurn
Head. Visibility was good, and there was no difficulty in making landfall
as planned. Although it was only a short distance to Driffield, there could
be no let-up on vigilance, until we were down and taxied off the flare
path. Jerry had a nasty sneaky habit of following aircraft in and firing on
the unsuspecting crew just as they were coming in to land. I had had to
spend the entire flight as second dickie, standing next to the pilot. It was
my first experience of operational flying. I thought, 'That was a piece of
cake! There's nothing to it.' I was soon proved to be very wrong.

Sometime later I was shocked to find out that the airfield we had
bombed was very near to the convent where my sister had been a pupil.
Although she was back in England, it was a nasty feeling to think that, if
our bombs had not been 'on target', we could have hit the convent! I felt
sick at the thought. Intelligence reports showed that, although most of
our bombs had fallen on the airfield, there had not been very much
damage to buildings and hangars. But that was the futility of night
bombing in those days. Not only was the training inadequate, but the old
bomb-sight was not all that accurate. It was difficult enough to hit a
target on practice, when the target was clearly identifiable, the weather
was good, and you could make a good steady run up to the target, and
fly with precision at the exact height, correct speed, and dead level,
without interference from flak. The experience that the aircrews had in
these early days of the war was, of course, invaluable to develop
precision bombing in the later stages of the bombing campaign, once
squadrons were equipped with the Lancaster, and the new bomb-sight.

Within the limitations of the bomb-sight and the inadequate training on
bombing, we had to do the best we could with Whitley Vs with Merlin X
engines – great lumbering crates. With a full load, you needed all the
take-off run you could get. They would get unstuck at about 85 knots,
and had a normal cruising speed of about 135 knots. However, they were
built as solid as rock and were capable of taking a lot of punishment. On
the other hand, if one engine failed, there was no time to look around

for a nice comfortable spot to make a forced landing, as I fully discovered later on. All the training we had carrying out emergency landings on Tiger Moths had very little relevance for these flying coffins. Still, we should not disparage the old crates, as they stood me in good stead on a few occasions.

The weather for the next fortnight was really foul, but we managed to get a few hours in between the storms, carrying out bombing practice, air testing and firing practice. By 18 July there was a break in the weather and we were briefed to attack Bremen.[3]

Bremen was much more heavily defended, so we had to do quite a bit of weaving to avoid the flak. It was not all that far inland and we had been briefed to avoid the most concentrated area of flak. We could easily get a pinpoint on the island of Texel off the Dutch coast, and with nearly a full moon and little cloud about we soon identified the target. Anti-aircraft fire over the target was a very heavy barrage but not very accurate, so it was a relatively 'easy' target. The round trip took six and a half hours.

The weather still held, so two nights later we were off again. This time the target was the aircraft works at Kassel. This was a different kettle of fish. To begin with Kassel was a lot further inland, so we were over enemy territory for over three hours. The town is situated on the river Fulda, but as there were several rivers in that area it was difficult to get a positive pinpoint. However, having got a good landfall on the Zuider Zee, if we flew from there on DR (dead reckoning), we should have had little difficulty in getting an exact ETA (estimated time of arrival) on the target. Provided the navigator had made his calculations correctly and the pilot flew dead accurately, we should have been spot on. We were. The bend in the river, north of the target, was easy to pick out in the light of the full moon.

At debriefing we could only say we had located and bombed the target. How accurate it was would be difficult to say, but, given that conditions were ideal, it was reasonable to claim a direct hit. Photo reconnaissance flights next day would show how much damage had been done. We landed back at base at 0400 hours. Dawn was just breaking and the fresh air outside was good to breathe. But, without doubt, the greatest pleasure was returning to the Mess and the smell of bacon and eggs greeting us. There has never been a meal that was so thoroughly enjoyable; lashings of bacon, eggs, sausages and tomatoes – it was certainly good to be alive.

It is interesting to note the No. 77 Squadron Operations Record Book (ORB) entry for this attack on Kassel, as history allows us to compare this with later raids that Richard took part in. The operational difficulties facing Bomber Command at this stage of the war are highlighted.

Sgt Coogan glided down from 1,000 feet [probably incorrect; this should be 10,000 feet] to 7,000 feet and dropped all his bombs in two sticks, the results were not observed. P/O North attacked from 5,000 feet and dropped the bombs in two sticks. The first stick was unobserved; the second stick struck the factory. F/O Meade was unable to locate the target so dropped his bombs on a railway and road near Wesel. F/Sgt Trewin arrived over the target at 8,000 feet but was unable to release his bombs owing to an electrical fault in the release mechanism. P/O Brownlie bombed from 10,000 feet and all his bombs fell in the target area. Sgt Deans attacked from 8,000 feet dropping his bombs in two sticks. The second stick hit the target and caused an explosion. P/O MacGregor reached the target area and found that his inter-communication had failed and therefore decided to return. On the return journey eight fighters (enemy) in formation were seen but did not attack. P/O MacGregor brought his bombs back to base as he did not see a suitable target and was unable to reach the primary objective. P/O Dunn made two attempts to start but was unable to do so owing to firstly engine trouble and the second time Wireless failure. P/O Piddington dropped the bombs from 8,000 feet, and saw one stick burst across the target, the second was not observed, but fires were seen to break out in the area. Fires were also seen near Munster. F/O Marks noticed a very large explosion near Munster on the return journey after bombing the target from 8,000 feet. His first stick overshot, the second burst across the target where a fire was seen to break out three minutes later. He located the target by picking up and following a railway which led directly to the factory. Most crews found the visibility fairly good, and all returned safely.

Three days later I started leave for what was to be the greatest day of my life. On 27 July I married that adorable petite, dark-haired, blue-eyed, vivacious girl with the fabulous smile. We had a week of glorious weather on honeymoon in Conway, and fourteen days' leave was over all too soon. We knew the chance we were taking when we decided to get married. Marie was well aware of the risks I would be facing, but at no time did she show any anxiety or fears for our future. When I boarded the train to return to the squadron, there were no tears as we waved goodbye, but her usual radiant smile to remember her by for the rest of my life.

Once more I was back to reality as I reported to the flight commander at Driffield, to be detailed immediately to do a daylight cross-country. The following day we were detailed for ops on Mannheim.

This was a much deeper penetration into enemy territory, and consequently we had to fly from an advance base at Mildenhall. Fortunately the route took us well south of heavy concentration of flak and we were able to pick up a good pinpoint on the river Mossel. The flight was uneventful, but we were airborne for seven hours fifteen minutes. We returned to Mildenhall for refuelling. I flew with a new skipper on this flight, Pilot Officer Brownlie, and stayed with him until the end of September, when I was made captain and given my own crew.

On 12 August we were given the aluminium works at Herringen near Eisenach, south-east of Kassel, as our target. There were no easily identifiable landmarks and there was not enough fuel reserve to stooge around to get a good pinpoint. The moon was about three-quarters, but there was a lot of cloud, which made it difficult to locate the target. This was one of those occasions when it was necessary to make up our minds quickly and let the bombs go as soon as we were reasonably sure we had got the target. The round trip took eight hours.

On 14 August, after only one night's rest, we were off again! This time we were required to hit storage tanks at the oil depot at Bordeaux. The moon was bright and visibility was good. The route over France was well clear of defences, so the flight was uneventful. In the bright moonlight, it was easy to pick out the mouth of the river Gironde. It so happened, however, that we were well off course, so we needed to get a good pinpoint. We were able to get a good landmark on crossing the French coast, where we made the necessary alteration to our course, and the navigator was able to get a very accurate estimate of the corrected wind speed and direction. This was to be a long flight, so we were instructed to use Hemswell as an advance base for refuelling. The round trip from Hemswell was eight hours. By the time we returned to Hemswell and had been debriefed, it was broad daylight and by that time we were past sleeping. We returned to base as soon as the aircraft had been refuelled, and we were back at Driffield in time for lunch.

One aircraft from No. 77 Squadron would fail to return that day. Flying

Officer William Stenhouse had managed to reach Bordeaux, but on the return to the English coast he decided to lose height and clear the cloud, trying to identify their exact position. The Whitley V struck the balloon barrage cables and crashed to earth near Eastleigh in Hampshire, with a total loss of life.[4]

We had finished lunch and retired to the anteroom for coffee. The wireless, which was located at the far end of the room, was giving out the news when I heard the air-raid sirens from the town of Driffield. At first, because our own station sirens were not sounding, no one appeared to take any notice. I was standing near the wireless and turned the volume down, so that everyone else could hear the sirens. This provoked a howl of abuse from my brother officers, who demanded that I return the volume to its previous level. I retorted: 'You chaps can stay here if you want but I am getting out.'

For a moment I hesitated, wondering whether to go out of the front of the Mess and get on my bicycle or to make a dash out of the east wing to the nearest air-raid shelter. In that moment the sound of Junker 88 engines was clearly audible. Instinctively I made for the shelter and I am quite sure that I would easily have qualified for the Olympic record, just as the first bombs were falling.

Jerry had evidently decided that No. 77 Squadron and No. 102 Squadron had been doing too much damage to the Fatherland and that it was time to teach us a lesson. Twelve Junkers 88s dive-bombed us, and taught us a master class in accurate bombing. No fighters had intercepted them, the local ack-ack batteries were useless, and our own station defences were quite inadequate. This consisted of one .303 Vickers machine gun perched on top of the water tower. The airmen manning this gun put up a spirited response throughout the attack but were totally ineffective.

We cowered in the air-raid shelter as several bombs fell uncomfortably close. After about a quarter of an hour we heard the 'all clear'. Emerging from the shelter to view the damage, we found that the Germans had done an effective job. One stick of bombs had fallen across the front of the Officers' Mess, and the west wing had been hit. My bicycle was a tangled mass of metal. I shall always be aware that, had I gone out of the front door instead of the east wing, I would probably never have written this narrative.

The damage was extensive. There were direct hits on three hangars and a direct hit on the airmen's quarters. In all, twelve men were killed, twelve aircraft were destroyed, and many other buildings were either destroyed or damaged.

We had been totally unprepared for this attack, and after the initial shock we wandered around in something of a daze to view the damage and to render what help we could where it was needed. We had not had any first-aid training or drills for such an emergency and we did not consider the possibility of any delayed-action bombs going off. A group of us came across an air-raid shelter that had received a direct hit. We passed by, thinking that there could not be any survivors in the shelter. Then I pulled myself together, and, when I came to my senses, my conscience told me to go back and help. I was totally unprepared for this sort of experience. When I got back to the shelter, a small group of fellows standing by said they thought there was someone still alive. The entrance to the shelter was completely blocked and the only access was down the emergency escape hatch. As I was fairly slim in those days, two of the others lowered me into the escape hatch.

This was my first real taste of war, and I was feeling just a little apprehensive, but once inside the shelter I looked around and, in the poor light, I saw, there in front of me, the body of an airman whose head had been squashed flat. I was surprised at my reaction on seeing this gruesome sight, for I felt absolutely nothing. He was dead. He felt nothing. I felt nothing.

RAF Driffield had been put totally out of action, and there was little we could do. The operation scheduled for that night was, of course, cancelled. On Sunday morning we set off by transport to Linton-on-Ouse, at 0830 hours, and were allocated new aircraft. We attended briefing at 1300 hours. There was no time for lunch, and at 1400 hours we flew to Abingdon, which was to be our advance base, and had a meal. We were scheduled to take off at 2030 hours.

The target was the aircraft factory at Milan (18–19 August 1940), Italy having entered the war in June. We had maximum fuel load, as this was going to be a long flight. There was no runway at Abingdon, so taking off needed extra care, but it was still daylight, and our skipper was an experienced pilot.

By the time we crossed the French coast it was already dark, but there was always the danger of night-fighters lurking around. There was quite a lot of cloud, which is always a welcome protection from fighters. Even so, much of the time we were flying on instruments, although occasionally we would break out of cloud into brilliant moonlight, when you feel you can be easily seen by fighters.

Climbing steadily to about 12,000 feet as we approached the Alps, we broke cloud cover. With the moon in the southern hemisphere, the mountains were sharply silhouetted, bleak, stark and foreboding. At that height it looked as if we were not going to clear the peaks. We identified Mont Blanc and the Jungfrau, and it seemed ages approaching, as the mountains were clearly visible from fifty or so miles. Black and menacing. As we passed over the highest peaks, although we cleared them by 1,000 feet, we seemed so close that it felt as though we could almost reach out and pick off a handful of snow.

Suddenly the whole scene was transformed. As we passed over the peaks, the snow-covered mountains were illuminated by the brilliant moon reflected by the dazzling white snow. The sight was quite breathtaking. It was as though the whole night had been turned to day. The reflection of the moon on the snow and particularly a glacier was a sight never to be forgotten.

We were roughly brought back to reality as our navigator called up on the intercom: 'ETA target 0030. Alter course 135 degrees. We have just passed over Lake Maggiore.' The target, an aircraft factory, was easy to pick out, and clearly illuminated by the brilliant moon. Neither was the flak a serious problem, but then, we thought, these were the 'Ities', and they were pretty clueless. There was no time to hang around, with the round trip taking nine and a half hours. The run-up to the target was straight, and the bomb-aimer called 'Bomb doors open?'

'Bomb doors open,' replied the skipper, and the bomb-aimer gave him directions.

'Right steady – left steady, steady – bombs gone.'

'Give me a course for home navigator,' requested the skipper.

'Three – one – five degrees skipper. ETA Base 0540.'

There was always a feeling of great relief when you got rid of your load. The prospect of landing with your bombs still on board was one that we did not relish. Also, on a long trip such as this, there was a natural tendency for relaxation. The skipper who had been at the controls for nearly five hours was bursting to pay a visit to the Elsan toilet for a pee. I took over and flew most of the way back. Flasks of coffee were brought out and some of the goodies were opened up; these usually consisted of one shilling's worth of confectionery such as a bar of Cadbury's milk chocolate, Rowntrees clear gums, a Kit-Kat, biscuits, glucose sweets and the like.

In those days 'George', the automatic pilot, was either unserviceable, unreliable or, what was more likely, not installed. So it meant being at the controls, literally flying the kite, all the time.

That night, when we returned to Driffield, the sirens went again, and we did not need to wait to make sure that we were the target once more. The Ju88s came back, with typical *Deutsch durchtigkeit*, to finish off the remaining two hangars, which they had missed on their previous visit. The standard of their bombing was remarkable, as they got direct hits on the remaining hangars. It was not too difficult, as we had absolutely no defences. The disruption of the bombing and strong winds prevented any further ops from Driffield, when it was decided to evacuate our squadron to Linton-on-Ouse on 28 August. As there was not enough room for another squadron to fly from Linton, we operated from the satellite at Tholthorpe.

No. 77 Squadron, RAF Linton-on-Ouse and RAF Tholthorpe

We were not given any time to relax as we were detailed to have a bash at oil storage facilities in Frankfurt on 2–3 September 1940. This was to be another eight-hour flight. The route would take us very near the Ruhr Valley – 'Happy Valley', as it became euphemistically known, where there were very heavy concentrations of defences.

The outward leg was routed south of the Ruhr, which should have taken us clear of the worst areas. Everything went fine, and we dropped our load and headed for home.[5] But, on this leg we were badly off course and went slap over Cologne. They waited until we were almost right overhead before opening fire, so we had no warning that we might have been approaching a danger area, and then they let us have it! We had the undivided attention of all the anti-aircraft batteries in and around Cologne. Searchlights were weaving all over the sky; they obviously did not have very accurate direction finding and seemed to be criss-crossing their searchlights aimlessly, hoping to pick us up by luck. The element of luck certainly played a big part in our survival on this night. Twice we were caught in a searchlight, but before others could join in the skipper had managed to weave out of the beam, constantly changing height, direction and speed. Heavy flak was bursting all around and some of it was uncomfortably close enough to smell the cordite and feel the force of the shell burst. I suppose the episode lasted only five or ten minutes, but it seemed a lot longer. It was a very uncomfortable five or ten minutes, and we were lucky that no vital parts had been hit. In fact, we had been struck in several places, and our aircraft was so badly damaged it was taken out of operational service. We made a precautionary landing at Misson near Retford, and were picked up by another aircraft and taken back to Linton-on-Ouse.

That afternoon I fixed up lodgings in Thirsk, so that my wife could come and stay with me. The RAF had a rule that married officers under the age of 25 would not be allowed to live out. I did not like that at all. So I requested an interview with the squadron commander, Wing Commander Jarman. I pointed out, very respectfully of course, that my marriage lines included vows that 'whomsoever God hath joined together in Holy matrimony, let no man put asunder', which in my opinion included the Air Minister. My wife and I fully realised that we were perfectly prepared to accept that I could be shot down at any time and that we naturally wanted to have what time we could together. Wing Commander Jarman was a jolly good type. He said that, as long as I was always available for duty whenever required and that my wife would not phone up to find out if I was coming home for supper, he would not object to me 'living out' and that it would be strictly 'off the record'. He pointed out that it was desirable for junior officers to spend as much time together off duty and on, in order to build up a strong bond of esprit de corps. However, as Air Ministry regulations had laid down that junior officers were not allowed to live out, I would not be eligible to claim living-out allowance. This was to prove to be a serious financial embarrassment in due course.

On 5 September we were detailed to bomb Turin, but we did not get far. Over the Thames Estuary one of the engines was overheating badly, and it would have been foolhardy to go any further. There was no alternative but to drop our load in the sea and get permission to divert to the nearest airfield. With one engine overheating, it was necessary to throttle back and fly on one engine. In a Whitley this was not a very nice experience, as it was very difficult to maintain height on a Whitley with only one engine. As it was, all went well and we landed at Wattisham.

While the Luftwaffe and the RAF fighter pilots killed and maimed each other fighting for control of the skies over England, a close eye was kept on German invasion preparations – Operation Seelöwe (Sealion). An assault on British shores would require the transportation of troops across the English Channel; air supremacy was paramount. The German Navy deemed it essential that the Royal Air Force be kept clear of the sea approaches to the south of England. Meanwhile, British intelligence maintained a vigil on enemy shipping movements across the narrow sea divide. The evidence was steadily mounting; for example, on 2 September 1940 Bomber Command Intelligence Report No. 904 reported:

> Photographs taken 1 Sep. show in southern four miles of South Beveland Canal 160 barges, 20 proceeding South, none moving North. Until 26 Jul. there have been no barges and no traffic in the canal and barge traffic considered abnormal. No unusual movement of barges in the Scheldt below Antwerp. No activity Flushing and Havre. No unusual feature in Boulogne.

On 3 September Bomber Command Intelligence Report No. 908 reported:

> Photographs taken 2 Sept. show: Off Calais thirty five small motor boats in line astern setting course northwest from neighbourhood Calais harbour. West of Dunkirk eight E boats in line astern proceeding west reported by visual reconnaissance four miles from shore. Increase of fifty barges Ostend since 31 Aug. Increase of one hundred and forty barges at Terneuzen since 16 Aug. No concentration of barges at the north end of Beveland Canal, slight increase since 1 Sept. at south end where total is now approaching two hundred.

And on 7 September Report No. 920 reported on photographs taken at 1130 hours that day, showing numerous concentrations in ports, including:

> Ostend: Increase of 100 barges making a total of 300. 30 vessels forty feet in length possibly tugs or motor boats for towing which are also new arrivals. Naval unit 280 feet long possibly coastal defence ship Peder Skram.
> Bruges – Ostend Canal: Six tows comprising 33 barges moving towards Ostend.
> Dunkirk: In harbour an increase of 45 barges total 75. No change in the barges in the waterways of the town. 32 barges anchored offshore.
> Calais: In the harbour are 86 barges, 13 smaller vessels probably for

towing and 35 small craft 45 feet. Lying off are 17 barges and 30 small vessels probably for towing.

Above are just a few of the intelligence reports on enemy shipping movements. Clearly something had to be done about it, and RAF Bomber Command was tasked with sinking boats and blasting port facilities. The bombing campaign against the build-up of enemy shipping in the Channel ports, the 'Battle of the Barges', proved instrumental in reinforcing the fact that the Germans needed air supremacy for a seaborne invasion. RAF Bomber Command played a prominent part fighting this battle, and many lost their lives.

On 7 September 1940 the Luftwaffe switched focus away from the RAF itself, believing, incorrectly, that Fighter Command's ability to defend was all but spent. The capital, London, became the target of a mass daylight raid, and that night further Luftwaffe raiders had no trouble finding the burning city and stoking the fires. On the evening of 7 September the code word 'Cromwell' was issued – invasion imminent.

On 8 September 1940 there was a big flap on, as reports came through that Jerry was preparing an invasion fleet of landing barges in preparation for landing their army on the south coast. If only Hitler had realised how weak our defences were, if he had gone ahead with an invasion, he could probably have succeeded. But he did not. We had to destroy those landing barges, which were assembling in the Channel ports. We were detailed to hit the harbour at Ostend. The weather was appalling, but it was one of those occasions when you did not let a little weather stop you. We had to fly through a lot of thunderstorm clouds, and the night was lit by spectacular flashes of lightning. The clouds were full of static electricity, which charged the aircraft and produced St Elmo's light. All the extremities of the aircraft, the propeller tips, the wing tips, glowed with a bright light. Ships at sea experience this phenomenon, which looks very pretty. It is the result of static being discharged quite harmlessly, but is nevertheless fascinating to watch.

I was standing beside the pilot, watching the propeller tips form arcs of light, lighting up the aircraft like a Christmas tree. As the lights grew, the noise of the static in the intercom also got louder, a crescendo. The lights were getting brighter when suddenly there was a blinding flash and a deafening crack. We had been struck by lightning. My immediate reaction was 'This is it, any moment now we will be falling out of the sky!' Instinctively I put my hand over my eyes, and uttered a prayer, 'Look out God, here I come.' After seconds passed, nothing had happened, and we were still flying straight and level. The skipper called up on the intercom, 'Everybody all right?' Each replied that he was 'OK skipper'. 'Let's press on then,' uttered the skipper.

Thunderstorms are usually fairly local and concentrated, so after a while we broke clear sky, just in time to see the coast coming up. We were able to pick out the target without any difficulty, sailed right in and dropped a stick of bombs right across the target and high-tailed it back home. On the way back the 'Wop' (the wireless operator) tried to get a fix and discovered that the trailing aerial had been burnt off by the lightning. Reeling in the aerial, he found a short length with a melted blob at the end! Had he wound the aerial in before entering the storm, as he should have done, the lightning would have passed through the aircraft somewhere else, where it could have had much more serious consequences. As it was, the lightning discharged harmlessly. That night, one of our aircraft was missing, believed to have gone down in the drink. Next morning every aircraft was sent to do a search of the North Sea. Each aircraft was detailed for a separate grid, in which each one would carry out a square search. It is unbelievable how difficult it is to pick out a yellow rubber dinghy in a vast expanse of sea. We had to fly at 1,000 feet, as there would be little chance of spotting anything from any higher. We continued the search for six hours, but saw nothing. There was always the possibility of encountering fighters, but with complete cloud cover we were reasonably safe. None appeared.

The night of 8–9 September 1940 was a busy one for Bomber Command, which sent 133 aircraft to targets at Hamburg, Bremen, Emden, Ostend and Boulogne. Eight aircraft failed to return from these operations, one of those being lost on the attack on the Blohm and Voss shipyards in Hamburg, with the Hampden crew of four all taken prisoner. Three Blenheims were lost on the Ostend raid and two Blenheims and two Wellingtons fell from the sky on the Boulogne raid. There was only one survivor from the crews lost attacking the Channel port targets. Twenty-six airmen had lost their lives. The bodies of five of these men were found and buried. The remaining twenty-one airmen were lost without trace, probably in the English Channel, their names commemorated on the Runnymede Memorial.[6]

Mid-week boredom was relieved by a camp concert called 'Bouquets'.

This was a quite excellent show organised by ENSA. The standard of entertainment provided by ENSA varied considerably. This was one of the better performances. The weather still remained very bad and ruled out any possibility of flying. Friday night, however, the weather lifted sufficiently for us to have another bash at one of the Channel ports. This time the target was Calais. We had to go in low, to get below the cloud base, which was about 5,000 feet. Once again it was quick in and out, and of course there was quite a lot of light flak. We could see by the scattered cones of searchlights and flak that there were several aircraft over the target at the same time, which reduced the concentrated attention on any one aircraft. With thick cloud cover the night was dark, but the target area was illuminated by the reflection of searchlights from the clouds. So Jerry made it a lot easier for us to find the target.

Saturday evening Geoff Wiltshear and I went into York and had a few drinks at the Florian. Geoff was slightly built and the quiet type, nothing brash or extroverted. He had only just had his 19th birthday. Sunday night the weather had improved and there was a full moon. We had another go at Ostend. This time we went in well above the range of light flak.

On the night of 18–19 September 1940 No. 77 Squadron lost two aircraft. A night-fighter attack sent Pilot Officer Eldridge's Whitley to earth in Holland with a total loss of life, and Pilot Officer Brayne's Whitley plunged into the sea on the operation to Antwerp. Two bodies were recovered, with the other three members of the crew having no known grave.[7] In total, Bomber Command lost nine bombers that night, with no survivors from the forty-one airmen manning these aircraft.

The rest of the week there was nothing doing. Geoff came with me to Thirsk, where I managed to get fixed up with lodgings for my wife. By the end of the week I had a back tooth removed, which had been giving me hell for several days. As I was hoping to find lodgings for my wife, some form of transportation would be essential. I spotted an advertisement for the ideal thing, a baby Austin Seven for sale, which I purchased for £17. It was a bit clapped out, but I was confident I could do it up and restore it to a reasonable condition. I spent every bit of spare time I had tuning the engine, cleaning pistons and valves, adjusting tappets and carburettor. The day I managed to get 55 miles per hour out of her was a great achievement.

Sunday, 22 September, we bombed a target at Dresden. We had been given strict instructions to avoid the centre of the town. Dresden was designated an 'open city' and as such was to be protected from damage. The target was on the outskirts of the city. There was still half the moon left, which made it easier to get a clear pinpoint on the river Elbe. The target was the marshalling yards. Bomber Command strategy was turning to dislocating the German transportation system, and, as Dresden was remote and thus less vulnerable, it became an important centre for distribution of industrial production in the area. Only the Whitley with overload fuel tanks and a reduced bomb load could do that range. The material effect on the outcome of the war, achievable by a handful of Whitleys at that range, and with the unreliability of accurate bombing, was doubtful. We operated from an advance base at Massingham near King's Lynn, and the trip back took nine hours and forty minutes.

The No. 77 Squadron ORB provides more details on the raid.

Whitley V – P4969 'H' P/O Brownlie, P/O Pinkham. Sgt Corlett.
Sgt Adamson, Sgt Hinde.
Duty – Attack on Lauta
Time up – 2015
Time down – 0555

P/O Brownlie arrived in the target area, which was located some eighty miles south east of Berlin, to find it obscured by cloud. He did suddenly locate it through a break, but, on returning, found it once more obscured, so he flew to Dresden, where he saw a train steaming into the main station. This he bombed, getting a direct hit, and wrecking a considerable section of it completely. The second stick he aimed at wharf buildings on the banks of the Oder [this should probably be the Elbe]. Very accurate fire was encountered at Dresden, Leipzig and Munster. He was forced down to 800 feet in order to get out of the searchlights.

We returned to Massingham for refuelling, and during the time we were being debriefed and having breakfast, the aircraft were being refuelled – at least so we expected. Unfortunately the skipper had failed to check the fuel gauges, and we set off for Linton-on-Ouse. The weather was beautiful, scattered strato-cumulus clouds at about 4,000 feet, and the prospect of a nice easy flight home. That is, until somewhere over

Lincolnshire, flying without a care in the world, when one engine suddenly cut, and a few moments later the other one cut. There was no time to look out for a suitably clear space to make a forced landing and from about 4,000 feet we dropped like two bricks! The skipper did the one thing he should not have done—namely, lowered the undercarriage. Landing on rough ground with wheels down could have had disastrous results. There was no time to fix my harness; all I could do was to brace myself as the pilot took the plane down on to some rough scrub land. We bounced along for hundreds of yards taking shrubs and small trees with us, hit a ridge with a ditch the other side, bounced over the ditch and gradually came to a stop. Apart from what appeared to be only superficial damage to the aircraft, none of the crew was hurt at all, other than being somewhat shaken. We got out, surveyed the damage, and just could not believe our luck. By all the laws of chance, we should have been completely wrecked. Fortunately, although it was very rough territory, at least being Lincolnshire it was flat country and there were no large trees or other obstructions. I never had to fly with that skipper again, as I was given command of my own crew and aircraft after that. Although I had been detailed to fly as second dickie with a sergeant pilot prior to this, but we had had to return after one and a half hours with engine trouble. We got back to base rather late, and I had to dash off to meet my wife, who had arrived at York.

She was looking as lovely as ever and greeted me with her usual radiant smile. She was not very favourably impressed with the baby Austin, but she accepted it was, as I told her, all we could afford. She gave it the nickname 'Mickey Mouse'.

We returned to Ouseburn, which was about 4 miles from Linton-on-Ouse and 5 miles from Tholthorpe, and settled into our lodgings. Strictly speaking the lodgings were for my wife. I would go and sleep with her only whenever I could get the time off.

Nothing happened for over a week. We spent the time doing air tests and standing by for briefing. Usually we were stood down just before midnight, so it meant hanging around in the mess all evening, which proved to be an absolute bind. At last it was announced that ops were on, and I was detailed to make my first op as skipper.

No. 77 Squadron suffered a further loss on the night of 23–4 September 1940, when Pilot Officer Andrew Dunn DFC was forced to ditch his Whitley into the North Sea following flak damage sustained during the attack on Berlin. The Royal Navy found two of the surviving crew four days later, but one would die shortly after the rescue.

The weather was terrible and we were briefed to bomb Rotterdam. It was pretty hopeless when we got to the target area, as cloud totally obscured the target, and, although we stooged around for ages, we were unable to find the target, the weather was so bad. We dropped our bombs on a target of opportunity. When we found a gap in the cloud, we picked a likely military target and offloaded. Not a creditable perform-ance for my first mission as captain, but with the appalling weather conditions it was the best we could do in the circumstances.

3. Skipper

No. 77 Squadron, RAF Topcliffe

On 5 October 1940 the squadron was moved to Topcliffe. This was a peacetime station, with comfortable quarters and a four-star Officers' Mess. We had to look for fresh lodgings near to the station, and we found an ideal cottage in a village in the country called Dalton. The lady was a typically friendly Yorkshire woman, and made us feel very much at home. She could not do enough for my wife, who soon made friends with the villagers, and life was very pleasant. The cottage was perched on the brow of a small hill and within about 6 miles of the airfield. As it was completely forbidden to have telephone contact with wives, because of the risk of careless talk, I was unable to let my wife know if I was down to fly on ops. Consequently she would not know if I would be coming home in the evening for supper. So we had a little understanding between us, that, if I was detailed for ops, I would fly low over the house when I carried out the usual air test in the morning. On one occasion I flew in from behind the hill on which the house stood, and below house-top level, and pulled up over the house with feet to spare. This frightened the life out of her, and when I realised how stupid it was she made me promise not to do it again. The slightest error of judgement and there would have been the most almighty prang.

Night after night she would hear the aircraft take off and count each one as it set course almost over the house. She would wait until she heard them returning, and count them again as they came in. If one was missing, she would have to wait one or two hours for me to get back to the house before she knew that I was safe. Almost the first thing she would ask when I got back was not 'Did you have a good trip?', but what chocolates, biscuits or anything else had I brought back. Very rarely did I consume more than the Rowntrees pastilles, as this was all I needed to keep my mouth moist. The rest I kept for her.

The night when we moved into lodgings at Dalton, 7 October, I was down to fly on a mission to Amsterdam. Once again there was thick cloud most of the way. We tried to get above it, but at 10,000 feet there were towering cumulo-nimbus clouds. At that height we had to put on oxygen. As we approached the Dutch coast, the cloud began to break and we could see ahead the flak and searchlights, which were giving a hot reception to some early comers. As there were many well-defined landmarks along the coastline, it was not too difficult to get a good pinpoint, and from there set course to the target. We had to mill around for some time before we were able positively to identify the target. The rear gunner said we had hit something. Sometimes it was difficult to differentiate between the flashes of gun fire and bomb bursts. But, as we would drop a stick of bombs, it was possible to see four or five flashes in a row. The rear gunner usually got the best view of the results, so the Intelligence Officer would place more credence on his report at debriefing. On this occasion we were credited with what was considered to be 'a successful mission'. The whole flight took six hours.

For the next fortnight we were constantly on 'stand by', and time after time 'stand down'. Although there was a full moon about 16 October, it was not until the 20th that we were told 'You're on tonight.' We had been hanging around for two weeks getting thoroughly brassed off. Whenever the weather eased up during the day, we would get some Z-Z practice in. If you had had plenty of practice at the blind flying beam-approach system, if your flying was really accurate, it was possible to make a landing in weather when the clouds were down to 200 feet. Only regular and frequent practice would make you sufficiently proficient to carry out this exercise. Consequently, whenever we had the opportunity, we went and practised Z-Z beam approaches and landing. So we were really glad to have a chance to have another go again.

This time the target was to be Weseling, near Bonn, just on the Rhine, south of the dreaded Ruhr Valley. Again the weather did not favour us. But, despite the amount of cloud, we had no difficulty in picking out the Rhine and located the target area. We encountered a lot of heavy flak, but the clouds protected us from searchlights, leaving the ack-ack gunners to rely on their direction-finding equipment, which fortunately for us was not all that accurate.

Richard's recollection of this raid is at odds somewhat with the No. 77 Squadron ORB, which reports:

P/O Pinkham arrived over the target at 6,000 feet prepared for the attack and then found that the bombs would not release due to a fault in the electrical releasing device. He was therefore obliged to return to base with the bombs on.

Richard recalls: 'Our bombs fell wide of the actual target but given the conditions it was not surprising.' Whichever was the case, it must have been particularly frustrating putting your lives at risk for either such a poor return, or indeed a failure to bomb. And to have to land a fully bomb-laden aircraft was not an easy task and very risky.

Four nights later I was on the raid to Kiel. Or, to be more precise, I should have gone to Kiel. Instead, I pranged my kite with another parked on the ground as I was taxying out for take-off. We had had a warning that there was a Jerry intruder in the vicinity, and all lights had to be off, except the very faint glim lights of the take-off flare path. I had my second pilot in the front turret with an Aldis lamp, with instructions to use it only very briefly. All navigation lights on the aircraft were switched off. But an aircraft parked near the perimeter of the aerodrome should have had lights under the wings, which would have been visible on the ground but not from the air. Proceeding very cautiously in the very dark night I did not see this parked aircraft and caught my wing tip on that one's wing tip. I could not have been more upset if it had been my own car. I felt sick. I got a good bollocking from 'Groupy' back in the ops room. But worse was to come. Air Ministry regulations stipulated that I was to receive an admonishing from the AOC at Group Headquarters. I duly reported in due course and was ushered into Air Commodore Cunningham's office. The office looked enormous and I felt very very small indeed. I marched in feeling very weak at the knees and threw the best salute I could manage.

'Stand at ease. Pilot Officer Pinkham?'

'Yes sir.'

'I understand you have been breaking two of my aircraft!' he said, with the emphasis on 'my'. I was mortified. That I should have broken two of his aircraft. I felt terrible.

'It is laid down in the King's Regulations that I have to admonish you. I herewith admonish you! Now come up to the wall map, show me where you have been and what you think of ops.'

'God,' I thought. I would go to the ends of the earth and back again for that man. Later I had to present myself before the station commander, Group Captain Hunter, who had the unpleasant duty of endorsing my logbook in red ink, 'Taxying accident 24/10/40 due to carelessness', signed J. Hunter Group Captain.

'We cannot have you doing the Jerry's job Pinkham, can we?'

'No sir.'

'You won't let it happen again will you?'

'No sir.'

On the 26th we were given a really dicey mission. The target was U-boat pens at Politz near Stettin. This was very nearly the absolute limit of our range, a distance of 660 miles. We seemed to be ages getting there. The route took us near several really heavily defended areas and particularly near Hamburg. They were most hostile, and we did not have sufficient fuel reserve to make any detours. Fortunately, however, we did not have any difficulty locating and bombing the target, and we did not hang around to see if any of our other kites had got there. The round trip took ten and a quarter hours. Thankfully we were stood down for three days to get over it. We had been on duty since nine in the morning, took off about eight in the evening, landing just about daybreak. After debriefing and breakfast I got back to the cottage about mid-morning, and by that time I was past sleep. By the time I went to bed I had been up for thirty-six hours. I got in some more Z-Z practice a couple of days later.

On 29 October the target was Magdeburg. The weather was very bad and the sortie was a total waste of time. We were in the air for nearly eight hours and saw nothing of the target. This was my eighteenth mission, more than halfway through the tour, but worse weather was yet to come. Most of the route over enemy territory was relatively free from defences. There was too much cloud so that the searchlights could not find us. From time to time they would follow our track and we could see the beams in the cloud. We passed well to the north of Hanover, out of harm's way. Even on a flight this long there was little conversation between the crew. I would call up the rear gunner.

'You all right Mike? Do you want to come forward to stretch your legs?'

'No thanks skipper. I'm OK.'

'How is our ETA Owen?'

'Should be over the target in about an hour. ETA, oh, one, three, five. Alter course, one one three.'

I pulled his leg.

'I think we ought to be another degree to port.'

'Don't you trust me skipper?'

'You need to sharpen your pencil.'

And so for ages there would be silence.

The squadron commander, Wing Commander Jarman, decided to come on the next trip with me, to see a bit of the action for himself. I did not know whether he wanted to have an opportunity to assess me personally, or if he was looking for a bit of excitement. We were detailed to have another bash at Italy, and this time the target was Turin. We went off early to operate from an advance base at Mildenhall. I was at the controls for take-off, and after normal take-off we climbed quickly to economic cruising height at 10,000 feet. The Wingco took over, and the flight over France was uneventful, but to clear the Alps we needed to climb to 13,000 feet. For some reason we were not getting full power and were unable to gain sufficient height. We thought that, as we used up fuel, we might have been able to climb further, but within sight of the Alps the Wingco decided we were not going to make it and turned back after flying for three and a quarter hours.

There is a further detail in the Squadron ORB concerning this sortie: 'W/C Jarman was forced to return owing to the fact that his aircraft could not be got above 13,000 feet probably due to icing. He returned with his bombs, and was heavily fired at over the Calais area.'

On 10 November we were detailed for Dresden again. The target was the large Sachsenwerk factory about 9 miles north-east of Dresden. The factory was well hidden in a forest with no good landmarks. All we could do was to head for Dresden and then set course north-east and find the target by dead reckoning. We stooged around for as long as I dared, without being able to find anything that we could identify as the target. I dared not spend any longer looking for the target, as we would have used up too much fuel. I decided that we would look for a secondary target, or 'target of opportunity'. Fortunately there was a full moon and it was not difficult to pick out the Elbe. The voice of the bomb-aimer yelled excitedly, 'Bomb doors open!'

'Left, steady – left, steady – steady – bombs gone!'

He had not waited for my OK. He said he had spotted a train steaming into Dresden and it was such a sitting duck he just could not miss the opportunity. We dropped a stick right across the track. The rear gunner confirmed that we had hit the train. The round trip took eleven hours! We got back to base feeling somewhat pleased with the result, but when we reported what we had done at debriefing we got a hell of a bollocking, for having dropped bombs near Dresden, as it was supposed to be an open city.

This was the period of the full moon, and with the better weather we took full advantage of the improved conditions. We were sent on four missions in seven days, all of which were long flights. On the twelfth we bombed a target at Weseling, a round flight of seven and a half hours. When we got back we learned that one of our squadron was missing, and I was shocked to find that it was Geoff Wiltshear's plane. It shook me badly, as we had become good friends. We discovered some time later that he had baled out and was taken prisoner of war. The rest of his crew had not survived. On 14 November we were detailed for Berlin and a flight of over nine hours.

The author of the Bomber Command Intelligence narratives had, for some time, been recording the effect of bombing on the morale of the Germans. Such 'good news' could inevitably be used as propaganda, perhaps, in some way, to offset the effect of the Luftwaffe attacks on British cities. Thousands of British civilians had already been evacuated to the country, away from the devastation, and those who remained chanced their luck, in shelters, tube stations or in their own homes beneath stairs and tables. The RAF had an important role in bolstering morale, showing that the war, at this stage, was not a purely defensive battle, and that Britain could hit back. It was important that the airmen believed they were having an effect. The Bomber Command Intelligence narratives, sent to all Group headquarters, kept the good news coming to the airmen, such as Richard Pinkham. Their long and dangerous flights over the Reich were not in vain.

Early in the war, the man at the head of the German Air Force, Reichsmarschall Hermann Goering, had stated publicly that no enemy bombers would be able to reach the Ruhr, let alone Berlin. Bomber Command airmen were going to prove him somewhat mistaken.

Bomber Command Intelligence Report No. 963
21 September. Berlin
It is reported that the recent bombing of Berlin has had an extremely bad effect on the population. Far from considering the raids as inevitable they feel they have been badly let down by their Government's repeated

assurances that no foreign aircraft could penetrate the defences.

It is further reported by a reliable source that the morale of the
people in Berlin is chiefly shaken by the bombing of the town itself and
also of the main lines of communication. This source also reports that a
number of high Party Officials left Berlin in a hurry and went to Upper
Bavaria for what they were pleased to describe as 'autumn holidays'!

Bomber Command Intelligence Report No. 1078
7 November. Political
The evacuation of children from Germany's more vulnerable areas
continues. A very large number are said to have been billeted upon the
inhabitants of Vienna. Foreign Observers have found morale to be at its
lowest in air raid shelters, where the authorities are being openly abused
for allowing the British raids – and the war – to continue.

On the night of 14–15 November 1940 RAF Bomber Command sent
eighty-two aircraft out on operational sorties against the enemy. The main
raid was against Berlin, to be carried out by fifty aircraft, including the
Whitley V T4169 'F' of Pilot Officer Richard Pinkham, taking off at 1715
hours detailed 'to bomb Stettiner Bahnoff Berlin'.

On this trip the flight commander, Squadron Leader Howard, came
with me. The night was clear and the moon was bright. Long before we
reached Berlin we could see fires that had been started by other waves of
bombers that had got there before us. We had been detailed to approach
from the south, making a dog-leg and leaving the target area flying
north. There was a heavy concentration of bombers on the target and
the one-way traffic was needed to avoid the possibility of collision. There
were fires everywhere. The ground was criss-crossed with sticks of
incendiary bombs, and the flak and searchlights were very dispersed, so
we sailed in with not too much attention being given to us. It was an easy
matter finding the target. We were lucky and hit it. Searchlights were
weaving all over the place, and every now and again one of our aircraft
would get caught and every searchlight would clamp on the poor bugger,
flak bursting around him, giving him a hell of a time, but as a result
taking the heat off us. We saw two of our kites go down in flames.

Of the fifty aircraft sent out by Bomber Command on this night to attack
Berlin, only twenty-five could later report reaching the city. Over the course

of the whole night the attrition proved high; ten aircraft we lost over enemy
territory, two ditched in the North Sea and one crash-landed in Norfolk.
Twenty-seven lives had been lost and a further twenty-one men would be
taken captive. No. 77 Squadron suffered; there was a total loss of life in
one 77 Squadron Whitley, and another ditched in the North Sea, the
crew, fortunately, surviving. The crew that lost their lives were piloted by
21-year-old Navy pilot Sub-Lieutenant Thomas Neal of the Royal Navy.
They are all now buried in the Berlin 1939–1945 War Cemetery. Neal had
flown with Richard Pinkham as second pilot on the raid to Magdeburg on
29–30 October.

Two nights later we were on again. This time it was to be Hamburg. This
was also a very heavily defended target. There was still a bright moon,
and it was easy to pick out the Elbe Estuary and make a short run up to
the target. This time we were getting a lot more personal attention, and
at times heavy flak got much too close for comfort. When the guns were
getting our range, we would just alter course, height and speed, so by the
time their range finders had got onto us, we were off in a different
direction. The problem was that, once you had committed yourself to
the bombing run, you had to hold everything steady while the bomb-
aimer had got the target clearly in his bomb-sight. After flying dead
steady for a couple of minutes, you could release the bombs and start
weaving like mad again. It would have been long enough for gunners to
get our range again, so that was the time to get the hell out of it. The
round trip took nine and three-quarter hours.

After four very long sorties in seven days, we were shattered and were
given fourteen days' leave and a very much-needed rest. Marie and I
packed our bags, stuck them in the back of Mickey Mouse and set off for
Southport to spend the fortnight at her parents' home. It was the first
time we had subjected the car to such a gruelling test – over the Pennines
in November. If it could cope with that, it could tackle anything. And it
did. It was really quite an achievement. We got to her parents' home in
time for an evening meal, and despite shortages and rationing Marie's
mother put on a very good meal. I never stopped to think how she did it,
but I realised later that she must have deprived herself. I was made to feel
like one of the family, although I had only met her parents three times
since I had first met Marie. On one occasion I had suggested to Marie
that I should take her to a performance of *La Traviata*, but she was not

very interested in opera, so turned down the offer. So I teased her, 'Well if you don't want to go with me I'll take your mother.' 'Suit yourself,' she retorted, so I took my mother-in-law. After that I could do no wrong in her mother's eyes.

We returned to the cottage at Dalton feeling refreshed and revitalised, and ready for the fray again. I suppose I never felt apprehensive about flying on ops. Some fellows were really scared; they were the real heroes. Those like me who did not really know fear were mad. But flying meant so much to me I never gave much thought to the dangers.

4. Not Likely to Forget

On 3 December 1940 Bomber Command sent out twenty aircraft to targets in Germany, with No. 77 Squadron's Pilot Officer Richard Pinkham at the controls of Whitley V P4299 'J'. Richard lifted his 'crate' at 1624 hours from the RAF Topcliffe runway, detailed to bomb the Mannheim central railway junction.

This trip was one I was not likely to forget. There was a full moon and cloudless sky and, at 12,000 feet, we felt naked and quite sure we could be seen by night-fighters from miles away. Mannheim is about 300 miles from the Dutch coast, and the route took us very near to some heavily defended areas. The total time over enemy territory would be about five hours, and, as this was one of the brightest nights, we had to be on a sharp look-out for fighters all the time.

There was a very strong tail wind on the route out, and to take full advantage we climbed to 14,000 feet with a wind speed of about 80 knots. We could always see the flashes of the heavy flak firing on the ground, so at that height a slight alteration of course would take us well clear of where the shells would burst. It would take several seconds for the shell to reach us after it had been fired, and it became something of a battle of wits between the gunners on the ground and us. When the shells burst well away from us, I just laughed and said, 'Missed again, you silly buggers!' We treated it very much as a game, the thought of them getting a lucky hit never occurred to me.

The moon was still high, casting a bluish-grey pearly lustre over the ground below. It was a glorious night; there was something surrealistic about the scene. It was this experience that I enjoyed about night flying. We continued on a course keeping well to the south-west of Cologne and other heavily defended areas. There was a very strong westerly wind, with at least a 10 degree drift; we flew on a course of 140 degrees. There was no difficulty in finding the target area. Mannheim is situated at the confluence of the rivers Neckar and Rhein, a landmark that stood out in the moonlight. The target itself was not so easy to pick out. We wanted to make positively sure we were absolutely spot on and not waste our bombs, so we stooged around for nearly an hour until we were certain we had identified the target. Even then, after taking so much trouble to be sure, we made a good run-up to the target – and missed! With the high wind, the bomb-aimer had possibly not allowed enough drift on his bomb-sight. It was probably a near miss, but we were certainly not spot on. Everything had been in our favour, good visibility, and a good steady run-up to the target, but we missed. Up to then, everything had gone fine, and we set course for home.[1]

Flying at 14,000 feet we had taken full advantage of the tail wind, but as this would be against us on the return flight I decided to descend to a level where the head wind would not be so strong. As the flak had not troubled us on the way out, I considered there would be no risk, and came down to 3,000 feet. I had the second pilot in the front turret map reading, and he gave me frequent pinpoints, and with the brilliant moonlight it was easy enough to pick out rivers, which gave me reassurance that we were right on track. We were aiming to cross the Dutch coast at the Schelde islands, which would have taken us well south of Rotterdam, but we were about 25 miles off track. I kept checking with the second pilot, and he assured me 'We're bang on track skipper.' Several times I checked with him and he seemed to be quite positive. A few more miles and we would be over the North Sea.

Suddenly, without any warning, every searchlight in the area fastened on to us. There must have been at least fifty. Instantly, all the guns opened up with light flak and tracer. It was coming at us from all directions! The inevitable happened; we got a direct hit in the fuselage. I really thought we had had it. But, blinded by the searchlights, all I could do was to get my head down, push the stick hard forward and, with nose well down, beat the hell out of it. This time Jerry was laughing at me. I thought that will teach me to have more respect for the Jerry gunners in future.

Somehow we were still flying under control, and there did not appear to have been any damage done to engines or vital controls. I kept the nose down until we were out of danger and out over the sea. I called up each of the crew in turn, to find out if they were all right, but Paddy the rear gunner replied, 'I'm all right skipper, I'm all right skipper', repeating everything strictly according to patter. 'I think I've been hit skipper – I think I've been hit.' Then, 'I don't think it has penetrated far. I don't think it has penetrated far. I can't see any sign of blood. I can't see any sign of blood.' Of course everyone could see the funny side of it, and roared with laughter. One could imagine poor Paddy bouncing up in his turret, feeling under his backside. 'I don't think it has penetrated far' conjured up images of blood gushing everywhere. I sent the wireless operator down to see him to see if he needed assistance; in the meantime I asked him if he could get out of his turret, but he replied, 'OK skipper, I'm all right!', again repeating it. But at least he did not sound distressed or in any agony. The W/Op came back, and reported that the fuselage was in a bit of a mess. As soon as we were clear of the Dutch coast, I handed over control to the second pilot, and went back to see for myself what damage had been done. A shell had burst in the fuselage, with holes everywhere. It looked like a colander. Still we were flying quite normally. I was astonished to find that the elevator control cables on the port side had been completely severed. Hopelessly I picked up the loose ends and contemplated the improbability of joining them, but, as we did not carry cable spares, there was no hope of carrying out running repairs. Glancing at the port side I was relieved to see that the duplicate set of cables was intact. I was naturally very concerned for Paddy, but, despite my entreaty for him to come out of his turret, he insisted on 'sticking to his guns'. He certainly did not appear to have been injured. The rest of the flight across the North Sea was uneventful. It was a beautiful night, with millions of bright stars, and the moon reflecting in the sea. This was the sort of experience that explained why I thoroughly enjoyed night flying. Recalling the ordeal of being caught in the searchlights and sustaining a direct hit seemed more like awakening from an all too realistic nightmare. We landed safely after having been in the air for ten and a quarter hours, but very thankful to be back on *terra firma*.

As soon as we landed, we examined Paddy's flying clothing, to find there were holes on both sides, which looked as if the shell splinter had passed right through his clothing. We piled into the dispersal truck, and lost no time getting back to the locker room to get Paddy's clothing off. Sure enough there were holes through his uniform trousers, but not a scratch on his skin. No wonder he thought, 'I think I've been hit. I don't think it has penetrated far.'

There were other instances of the Whitley taking a hammering. There was one occasion when the whole of the side of the fuselage was blown out, so by comparison we got off lightly.

After that hair-raising experience the weather clamped down and we were stood down for the whole week. December in Yorkshire when the weather is bad can be miserable. We were more than grateful that we had the comfort of a peacetime Mess, with the leather-upholstered 'club' easy chairs and a large warm fire. But as soon as we were stood down I would head straight for Dalton village and the joy of being able to spend the night with Marie. We grasped every possible minute together. Although our landlady was kindness itself, the coal ration was very meagre, so we would huddle together in front of the fire to keep warm, until the last dying ember of fire had gone and we would go to bed.

We returned to Mannheim on 10 December 1940. Although the weather had improved slightly, it was still very grim. The forecast promised good weather over base for take-off and return, and possible clearance over central Germany. So once again we were briefed to go to Mannheim. I think that, as we had not put up a very good show last time, it was decided we should go again and finish off the job properly. This time the weather produced the worst conditions I ever experienced. There was heavy cumulo-nimbus cloud halfway across the North Sea up to a height well above our maximum. We continued climbing to get above it without success. Then the thing that most pilots dread the most – we were in icing conditions. We were first made aware of this by the loud bangs on the side of the fuselage. It took a while for it to register that this was chunks of ice breaking off the propellers. The Whitley was well equipped to cope with icing conditions. There were 'slinger rings' that ejected de-icing fluid along the propeller blades; also hot air for the carburettor air intake, a pitot-head heater, and a pulsating rubber leading edge on the main and tail plane, to prevent ice building up on the wings. We activated all these devices, and, although the carburettor air intake heater caused a reduction in power, it was not significant. So we kept going, hoping we would soon come out of the cloud and icing. It was not long before the air-speed indicator packed up. Evidently the pitot-head heater either was not adequate or broken down up completely. All other instruments were functioning, so I relied on maintaining height with the altimeter, constant engine power and the climb and glide indicator. So long as I kept the height constant, we should maintain a constant speed. We continued in these appalling conditions fully expecting to run into clear weather near the target. We carried on like this for two hours. There was always the possibility that, if we had come down lower, the temperature might have been above freezing, but this involved risks of the unknown. We reached the target area on ETA still in cloud. We dropped our bombs on ETA and turned for home. It was not until we were well over the North Sea that I decided it was safe to descend. As soon as we got below 5,000 feet we were out of cloud and icing. The pitot-head thawed and so our air-speed indicator started functioning again, and I was back on normal instrument flying once more. Conditions back over England were quite good, with broken strato-cumulus, below which visibility was satisfactory. We got a good pinpoint on the coast and set course for base. We soon picked up the flashing beacon and the airfield glim lights shortly came into view. It was a wonderful sight to see the flare path, and we got an immediate 'green' from the aerodrome control, completed a circuit and made our final approach. As you descend on the approach leg, the flare path lights appear to level out, so you get a feeling of great relief with another 'mission completed'. We touched down safely eight hours after take-off.

I made a practice of being among the first aircraft to take off on most ops, and on 12 December I was first off. There was a bit of mist about and the flare path was illuminated with goose-neck flares. These were cans with long necks containing paraffin and a large wick. When these were lighted, they gave off quite a lot of light, but they would not be used if there was any sign of enemy aircraft in the area.

The sky above was clear and the weather forecast was good, but with early morning mist. So the sooner we got off the sooner we would be back and hopefully before the mist started to thicken. In those days, with the elementary equipment and lack of practical experience, we could not blame the Met for getting it wrong occasionally. It was no discredit to them with their limited forecasting resources. This was one of those occasions when they got it wrong. Unfortunately, as I had been first off, I had got furthest from base when, not more than forty minutes from take-off, we got a recall signal. Consequently I would be the last to land. The mist was developing much faster than had been expected, and we had to get back before visibility clamped down. The mist was closing in fast and by the time we were back over the aerodrome the mist was really thick. In the meantime the aerodrome duty crew had already set out and lit paraffin flares. These were not the goose-neck type but large buckets full of paraffin and with enormous 'wicks'; the glow from these bucket flares could be seen from a considerable distance, even in quite foggy conditions. From above you could see only this glow, which you could home in on. The technique then was to do a timed circuit, flying on accurate bearings, line up with the flare path and make a steady rate of descent, so that by the time you were over the airfield boundary you should be able to see the flare path and land. It called for precision flying, and with a bit of luck you made it first time. There was a tendency to hold off too high over the flare path, as the lights gave the illusion that you were nearer the ground than you should be. I said a quick prayer to St Christopher (I always carried a St Christopher medallion) and plonked her down, a bit bumpy but safe. 'Thank you St Christopher!' I uttered.

With Christmas near I was hoping for a spot of leave, but with the weather generally so bad we had to operate whenever there was a chance. The weather had to be good for take-off, over the target and for landing on return, although frequently we would be diverted to another aerodrome if the weather had closed in over base. During the winter months these opportunities did not occur very often. On 21 December we were briefed to do Merseburg.

Merseburg meant deep penetration into Germany, not far from Leipzig. If all went well, it would be an eight-hour round trip. We were routed to avoid heavy concentrations of flak, and most of the way we saw very little, but, as might have been expected, it was fairly concentrated over the target area. We knew we had got there by the flak and searchlights. We made a straight run up to the target, which we were able to pick out from the light of flares that had been dropped by aircraft that had already got there. We were credited with having hit the target.

Once again we were in trouble. On the way back the radio packed up. This was not a serious handicap if the weather was favourable and we could get some good pinpoint landmark on the coast. But, if the radio went u/s and the weather was bad, then you would be in trouble. This time we were in real trouble. The weather had deteriorated badly as we approached the English coast, so we were unable to get any more pin-points, and when we crossed the coast on ETA we could not see anything. We flew on further until our estimated position was over base. There was no sign of the flashing beacon; at least we could not see it through the cloud. I came down to about 2,000 feet, which was the safe minimum height for that part of the country. We could not raise any response on

R/T. In short we were lost! Up sh** creek! Not a light of any description. We circled around calling 'mayday' on R/T, but no one seemed to hear us. I dared not risk coming down below 2,000 feet, as we could have drifted miles off course, probably somewhere over the Pennines. We fired off a red Verey light but that brought no response. 'God knows where we are!' But just then one of the crew spotted a light on the ground, and I started circling round it. Then another light appeared, then another and another. A row of lights, not altogether straight but obviously intended to be a flare path of some sort. Someone had heard us circling around, someone cared and decided we needed help, and had laid out a landing strip with goose-neck flares. Eventually we were given a 'green' on an Aldis lamp and we made our final approach. Down to about 200 feet on our approach something flashed past our starboard wing. I thought, 'My God. What was that?' We landed safely and were given a very warm welcome. It was well after midnight, but some chaps had been drinking late in the Mess, when they heard us circling above and realised we were in trouble. We had landed at Yeadon near Leeds, 26 miles south-west of base. There were peaks of 1,700 and 1,830 feet just 20 miles further west. It would have been suicide to come down below 2,000 feet. Next morning when we went out to our aircraft we saw what it was that had flashed past our wing – an enormous chimney just off the line of our approach last night. Our thanks again to St Christopher. That sortie had taken nine hours. By now I was wondering if my luck could possibly hold out. That had been my twenty-seventh sortie, and I had three more to do to complete my tour of ops. You could not help wondering if it would be your turn next, although I never really thought I would be one of those who would have 'bought it'!

We were stood down over Christmas, which gave us the opportunity to relax and unwind, but air testing went on just as usual during the daytime. The day after Christmas I was detailed to give my kite a thorough air test in preparation for the next sortie. This was to be somewhat different – mine-laying in the estuary off the Gironde. We had to have the bomb-bay modified to carry one mine.

On 27 December 1940 we were sent to Bordeaux. The estuary was easy enough to find, but we had to go in at about 500 feet and drop down to 300 feet to release the mine. Unlike the 'Dambusters', we did not have any special training for this, but it was absolutely necessary to plant the mine precisely. In fact the mission was pretty dicey, as the estuary was well defended, with flak coming at us from both banks of the river. The searchlights did not bother us too much, as at that height the beam is very narrow, so it was not easy to pick up a low-flying aircraft. We flew up the estuary for about 20 miles before dropping our load. Although we were in the target area for only about eight minutes, it is amazing how long eight minutes can seem. The moon was in its last quarter, but visibility was good, so we had no difficulty in finding the dropping spot. We operated from Abingdon as an advance base, and landed back at Abingdon having done another nine-hour flight. Although the return flight was over France, most of the way there was no chance of relaxing, and the crew had to be on the alert all the time. We left the French coast with the Cherbourg peninsula to our port, giving us a very easily identified landmark. An hour and a half later we were back over Abingdon, having been airborne for nine hours. Nine hours on the alert, concentrating on the flying instruments, the navigator keeping his log in detail, the wireless op keeping a listening watch, the rear gunner being on the look-out for fighters, and the second pilot checking instruments and noting landmarks, give little opportunity for relaxing. So, by the time we landed we were very pleased to have a cup of hot soup while we were being debriefed and get to the Mess for breakfast, of bacon, eggs and sausages. That was really good and put new life into us. We did not sleep, and as soon as the aircraft had been refuelled we set off back for base. We preferred to return to base as soon as possible to get back to our own quarters for sleep and to knock back a few pints. Then we were ready for anything.

On 2 January 1941 we were on again, and this time the target was Bremen. This was one of the most heavily defended targets, but there was no opposition until we got to the East Frisian Islands, which gave us a very good landmark, from where we could set course for the target. From that point we were harassed all the way to the target. We picked up another good pinpoint at the mouth of the Weser, and from there it was only a matter of about ten minutes to the target. But that ten minutes seemed like an hour. The heavy flak was very concentrated, as were the searchlights, but we managed to evade them. Shells were bursting very close to us and at times giving the plane a hefty jolt, but nothing got near enough to do any damage. Constant weaving kept us just out of harm's reach. There was no need to stooge around to find the target; it was clear enough as we made a direct run-up. We lost no time in high-tailing it out of the danger as soon as we had dropped our bombs. From there on there was no flak, and we were soon out over the North Sea again.

So far the weather had been quite kind, but, although it had been good on take-off, no sooner were we on our way back than we got a diversion signal from Group Operations control: diverted to Charmy Down. Weather in the north had clamped down, and in fact it was pretty bad throughout the country, except for Charmy Down in Berkshire. This was one of the few airfields in the country where conditions were reasonably good. As Charmy Down was only a satellite airfield, there were no facilities, so we had to fly on to Abingdon, where we had to stay the night until the weather had cleared up north.

Marie had waited all day not knowing that I was safe, but it was not possible to let her know that we had had to be diverted. It was not until Saturday afternoon that I was able to get back to our lodgings, much to her relief. If she was ever anxious, she never showed it, putting on a brave face at all times. She used to say that if ever I got shot down she would rather I was killed outright; she dreaded the thought of me being taken prisoner of war. One more sortie and my tour would be finished.

I had to wait a whole month before the weather was good enough to do a sortie. We spent the time whenever the weather permitted doing Z-Z practice and formation flying. Not that we ever expected to fly in formation on ops! But it was something to keep us from getting bored.

Marie and I were invited out on a few evenings for bridge, which was a very pleasant change. We both enjoyed playing bridge, but had difficulty in finding another couple to make up a foursome.

Eventually the weather lifted on 10 February, and we were briefed for Hanover. The route was over territory that was clear of flak, but we had to be very much on guard for fighters. There was a lot of cloud, and, with a full moon illuminating the clouds, it was a magnificent sight, as we flew just above the tops of the clouds most of the way.

By the time we reached the target area most of the cloud had dispersed, and we got a pinpoint of a lake just west of Hanover. We received quite a lot of attention from flak over the target, but it was by no means as troublesome as some of the other targets we had previously been to. After we had left the target area, it was a piece of cake, with no interference from flak, the route taking us well clear of heavily defended areas. The rest of the flight was uneventful – that is until we crossed the Yorkshire coast, and some light-fingered ack-ack gunners started firing at us. We were hardly expecting that sort of reception, and as luck would have it they were not very good shots. We soon put a stop to that nonsense and fired off a 2-star Verey identification flare. That gave us a few bad moments. After seven hours we touched down safely. We were credited with hitting the target.

That was my thirtieth op and the end of my tour. I got a weekend pass to take Marie back to her parents, as her mother was ill. I returned to Topcliffe, and Marie came back by train a week later. There was an Officers' Mess dance on Saturday and I celebrated the end of my tour rather too well. A few days later I was given fourteen days' posting leave prior to being posted to No. 10 OTU Abingdon for duty as a staff pilot. At the end of my tour I had clocked up 530 hours total flying. I was quite looking forward to returning to Abingdon and to having Marie with me, and the prospect of war summer months after the miserable cold weather we had had in Yorkshire.

Richard's first tour of operations was over. Statistically his chance of surviving this tour was just below one in two (see Appendix 3). On thirty occasions he had gone 'over the top'. History would show that the damage caused by the raids on Germany at this stage of the war had very little material effect, although it was proof that the Royal Air Force was fighting back. The raids on the Channel ports, in opposition to the German mustering of seaborne invasion vessels, had, however, damaged the enemy in material and strategic terms. On 17 September 1940 the German Navy expressed its concern that 'the RAF are still by no means defeated: on the contrary they are showing increasing activity in their attacks on the Channel ports and in their mounting interference with the assembly movements'. On 21 September the German Navy recorded that 21 transports and 214 barges had been taken out of action by the Royal Air Force. Eventually the further assembling of invasion barges was suspended along with the dispersal of those already part of the invasion fleet, 'so that the loss of shipping space caused by enemy air attacks may be reduced to a minimum'.[2] Bomber Command's airmen, men like Richard Pinkham, proved to the German Navy that air superiority was essential for a cross-Channel invasion. The Luftwaffe failed to achieve this, and Hitler's aggression was diverted. Bomber Command's 'Battle of the Barges' was an essential element in the defensive victory that was the Battle of Britain.

5. A Respite – of Sorts

Most operational Bomber Command crews spent time at an Operational Training Unit (OTU) prior to a posting to front-line squadrons. In August 1939 thirteen squadrons had been tasked with training aircrews up to operational standard, and in April of the following year these were designated as OTUs. It was a time when experience could be gained flying as a team, in preparation for entering the air war. Into such OTUs were posted tour-expired aircrew, who could then pass on their operational know-how. These novice instructors, usually in their early twenties, could then guide the novice airmen. It was perceived as a period of rest for the tour-expired flyers, but it was certainly not a risk-free environment, and thousands of airmen, trainees and instructors, would lose their lives in accidents, before they had even ventured into enemy skies.

No. 10 Operational Training Unit, Royal Air Force Station, Abingdon

I set off from Southport to Abingdon in my baby Austin, but broke my journey and spent the night at Leamington Spa. Despite the car being ten years old it was a marvellous little tub and never gave me any trouble. I arrived at Abingdon on Saturday morning and reported to the adjutant. Nobody was particularly concerned about me arriving on a Saturday morning, so I got fixed up with a room and settled in.

I was very lucky to find lodgings in Abingdon and sent a telegram off to Marie, for her to come and join me a week later. In the meantime no one seemed to be in much of a hurry to get me started, and it was not until the end of March that I was detailed to take my first aircraft with a crew under training.

I was attached to 'A' flight on Whitleys, which I was particularly delighted to find were Mark Vs with Merlin engines. The previous time I had been at Abingdon they had had Whitley IIIs with Armstrong

Siddeley Tiger VIII radial engines. I had not relished the thought that they might still have had those old crates, having got used to the Merlin on ops.

There were very few familiar faces still at Abingdon, since I had last been there. After a couple of evenings at the 'Doghouse' pub I soon got integrated with the rest of the fellows. Sunday, the 23rd, was the King's National Day of Prayer, which was celebrated with a full church parade. Marie arrived on Monday. I picked her up at Oxford, where we had lunch, and took her along to our lodgings in the afternoon.

Later that week I had the unenviable task of representing the officers and men of the station at a funeral of one of our aircrew members, who had been killed in a crash; his body was taken to his home town for burial. The funeral took place at Sevenoaks, and he was given full military honours. The service was very moving, and the sounding of the Last Post and firing the salute volley over the grave sent cold shudders down my spine. Then I had the heart-rending task of expressing the sympathy of the Officer Commanding RAF Abingdon to the wife, parents and relatives. I was shocked that the wife did not seem to be in the slightest bit upset. I suppose the reality of the tragic loss had not really sunk in, or she had developed a psychological blockage.

I returned to Abingdon to find preparations going ahead for a dance in the Officers' Mess. As this was a non-operational station, such social activities were less inhibited. The station had its own dance band, which was really quite good. The entrance hall, lounge anteroom and dining room were decorated with lovely flowers and it was good to see so many girls in beautiful gowns. The evening was a great success, the only regret being that it did not go on long enough. These formal occasions were most enjoyable and exhilarating; unfortunately wartime restrictions excluded the wearing of full Mess dress kit.

The night following the dance I was detailed to fly on a night cross-country with a trainee crew. The prospect of doing a night cross-country with an inexperienced crew was not a pleasure to which I particularly looked forward. I prepared my own flight plan, and knew at the worst that I should be able to find my way home if the navigator got us lost. I had that little confidence in the crew's competence. All went well on this first flight, which lasted four hours, and we landed before midnight, which was not too tiring.

While we were living out, we had the advantage of obtaining all our groceries from the NAAFI store, and I was pleasantly surprised when the store man, to say the least, was rather generous in the portions he served. Marie was even more pleased when she saw what I had brought home. At least the prospect of our stay at Abingdon was very favourable, as far as food was concerned. Saturday we had a free afternoon and Marie and I went into Oxford. We were now entitled to a living-out allowance, which eased our financial situation considerably, though I was still on a Pilot Officer's pay, which did not let us go hectic.

For the next ten days I was flying fairly frequently, although daytime was usually local flying, and practice bombing, with cross-country flights at night. I was then transferred to 'B' flight to fly Avro Ansons, with very inexperienced trainee navigators and wireless operators. I cannot say I was ever very fond of the Anson. It was a very stable aircraft, and generally considered to have one of the best safety records in the Air Force. It was a bit antiquated – the undercarriage had to be wound down by hand! Still there was more room to move about in the fuselage, and that is what mattered more for the purpose for which it was being used. Most of the time we were doing some pretty intensive flying, often one flight in the morning, one in the afternoon and one at night. Sometimes we might do one cross-country in the day then two cross-countries that night.

During the first fortnight in May the pace hotted up even more as the better weather developed. The pressure was on to get crews through training as quickly as possible to replace losses on the squadrons. At the same time more and more aircraft were coming off the production lines, building up squadron strengths. Most of the flights in May were daylight cross-countries, and I soon began to recognise prominent landmarks. There were the brick kilns at Bletchley, which on some days belched out smoke across the country for 50 miles or more and which could be seen from many miles away. There was Savermake forest with its unique triangular shape. Most of the cross-countries were over the West Country. These landmarks became so familiar and easy to identify that I did not mind if the trainee navigator did get us lost – I was not. By June we were doing many more night cross-countries.

By the end of June I started suffering from severe headaches in the back of my head. With every footstep I took, it felt as if someone was bashing my head with a mallet. I reported sick and was sent to Oxford Royal Infirmary to the ENT specialist on 2 June.

I reported to the chief instructor, who said he had no time for anyone who was sick, and as good as implied that I was LMF, which meant having Lack of Moral Fibre, a term applied to those who refused to fly without a good medical reason. This was a very serious allegation if it could have been substantiated. I was incensed and very indignant. I just could not believe how he could have accused me of LMF.

I was given a week's sick leave. We went to Witham, my home town in Essex, for a few days. When we returned to Abingdon on the Sunday Marie became unwell. I had to report to the specialist again on the Monday. On Thursday, 10 June, I was sent off to Torquay for a spell at the RAF hospital. So I put Marie on the train for Southport.

The RAF had taken over the Palace Hotel, to be used as a convalescent hospital. In those days it had been a five-star hotel, and, apart from medicine, physiotherapy and psychotherapy, it was in every respect like having a luxury holiday, but at the Royal Air Force's expense. The regime was very easy going, and we were allowed out to go anywhere, provided we were back by ten o'clock every evening. I had a couple of sessions with the Medical Officer, who 'sentenced me' to hard physical exercise. Not having done any serious exercise since I was down at Hastings on the disciplinary training course, it came as something of a shock to my system. After a few days, I thought they were trying to kill me! Every muscle in my body ached like hell. The worst 'torture' was heaving an 18lb medicine ball around. I had to keep this programme up for the whole seven weeks I was there.

I had two sessions each week with the shrink, Wing Commander Gillespie. I was put through psychology tests, and, as far as I could see, he did nothing else. But he did go out of his office on one occasion, and needless to say I took the opportunity to sneak a look at his notes on his desk. There was one comment that hit me. I was too 'self-centred'. Then I became aware of all the other patients, many with limbs missing, or in plaster casts, some with bad burns on face and hands. One chap who had only one leg went swimming daily in the hotel pool, and it was when he was diving off the top diving board that suddenly I realised what Wingco Gillespie had meant. I realised I was too much concerned with my own problem, when there were many who were far worse affected, and who were not feeling sorry for themselves. From that moment on, I gradually got over my severe headaches.

It was permitted for wives to stay near the hospital, so I found lodgings nearby, and Marie came down to Torquay. I was allowed to see her every day, but we were not allowed to sleep together. I had to be back in my room by ten o'clock. We spent many enjoyable times swimming, dancing and going to shows. There was a nine-hole approach and putt golf course in the hotel grounds. We had a trip up the river from Dartmouth to Totnes, and many other thoroughly enjoyable outings. The profound impression of my stay at the hospital was of all the other patients all accepting their disabilities with such fortitude.

One such man was the pilot who had suffered the distinction of being the worst burnt case to have survived. My reaction on first meeting him was one of utter horror. His face was horribly disfigured. When I first met Flying Officer Edmunds it was impossible to look at him without a feeling of extreme horror. No words can describe the severity and extent of his injuries. And yet he had the most terrific spirit, and with such a wonderful personality very soon this quality of his character completely eclipsed his disfigurement. In due course fate was to bring us together again and we were to become good friends.

After seven weeks' convalescent stay at Torquay I returned to 'flight duties'. I was desperately anxious to get back on flying again, but the headaches had not cleared away. I was grounded pending the result of a Medical Board. I attended for a medical at RAF Hospital Halton on 16 September and was categorised 'A2hBh', which meant I was fit for flying, home service, and limited to a maximum of 5,000 feet. During all this time I was put on permanent ground duties and became Aerodrome Control Pilot. That is the chap who stands at the end of the runway to flash a red or green light on the Aldis lamp, for aircraft about to take off or land.

Even in the autumn months it used to get very cold at night. At least we were not required if it was raining. I was doing ACP duty one night when we got a mayday signal from an aircraft in trouble with engine failure. I had given him a 'green', and he was on his final approach but appeared to be too low. The next moment, when he was less than a mile from the end of the flarepath, he went straight in. I never heard the result of the Court of Inquiry, but it would have appeared that he had let his speed drop and stalled. I continued to do ACP duties almost every night for the rest of October and had my first flight again on 26 October, after being off flying for three months.

It is likely that this is the No. 10 OTU Whitley lost on 24 October flying from nearby Stanton Harcourt. The pilot, Flight Sergeant C. E. Levitt, was killed, along with his crew of three. In W. R. Chorley's *Royal Air Force Bomber Command Losses Volume 7: Operational Training Units*

1940–1947, the author records a report from a Pilot Officer Gibbs to the Chief Technical Officer (Wing Command Holder) at No. 10 OTU.

Whitley V P5023 with F/S Levitt as Captain took off from Stanton Harcourt at 0105 hours. Soon after a mist began to settle down over the aerodrome and the aircraft was given a 'green' to land. Making a circuit, the aircraft lost height and was seen to go up in flames. On investigation at the scene of the crash, the aircraft struck the top of a high tree (approximately 60 foot) with the port wing. The outer portion of the wing was torn off at the points of attachment leaving the wing tip in the top of the tree. From marks on the wreckage and the tree it would appear the aircraft was banking to the left, this together with the force of impact and the loss of the wing caused the aircraft to roll over to the left and crash in the inverted position. The aircraft caught fire and was immediately burnt out. From the little that was left of the aircraft, it was possible to ascertain that the wheels had been locked down but the flaps were still up. One airscrew blade was still attached to its hub and this blade was in fine pitch. The aircraft had flown 187.03 hours. Port engine 148462 51.45, starboard engine 148440 52.45. The aircraft was placed Category E.1.

No. 1481 Target Towing and Gunnery Training (TT & GT) flight, RAF Goxhill

I was posted to Goxhill on 3 November 1941. Nobody had ever heard of Goxhill. Nobody had the slightest idea where it was. Eventually we found it on the map, miles from anywhere, in a remote spot in north Lincolnshire, near Hull. Banished! The RAF had no use for me any more! The postagram gave no indication as to what was the posting, or what my duties were to be. I arrived at Goxhill on 5 November. I was quite convinced that I had been 'banished' to this remote isolated place for having upset the chief flying instructor at Abingdon. He did not like me. He believed I was malingering. The fact that I had completed a whole tour of ops on Whitleys did not seem to count with him.

I arrived at Goxhill to find the place almost deserted. All I could see was a solitary Tiger Moth and a couple of Nissen huts. I made my way to the Nissen huts, where I saw half a dozen 'bods' standing around supposedly with nothing to do. A flying officer came over to greet me and ushered me into an office. There I found a table and a chair. There were some papers on the table. Then, much to my surprise, one of the

chaps turned out to be Flying Officer Edmunds. We were both delighted
to renew our acquaintance.

'Jock' was seated at the table, a stocky Scot flying officer. I told him,
'I've been posted to Goxhill. Where do I sign in?' I added, 'I had better
report to the CO. Where is he?'

'He has not arrived yet,' Jock replied.

'Do you know where he is?' I queried.

'Here's the postagram.' Jock pointed to the papers on the table.
'There's a chap named Flight Lieutenant Pinkham posted as CO.'

'You must be joking,' I exclaimed. 'That's my name, but I am not
a Flight Lieutenant.'

'See for yourself. See the postagram. That's your name all right.
Thank God you've arrived at last. Now we can get cracking.'

'Just a minute,' I said. 'I've had no instructions. What are we supposed
to be doing?'

Jock, who had some idea, said, 'We have got to form a Target Towing
and Gunnery flight. Do you know anything about it?'

'Not a clue,' said I.

'That makes four of us,' one of the others said.

'Typical,' said another fellow. 'Nobody tells you anything in this
crazy outfit.'

That evening we got to know each other very well, celebrating my
promotion. The following day, for want of something to do, and to let
the others see I really could fly, and also to satisfy myself that I had not
lost my touch, I took the Tiger Moth up and did a few aerobatics. The
next day I decided to fly to Binbrook, to find out what was supposed to
be going on.

On 10 November we were all transferred to Binbrook. The next day I
had to report to the RAF hospital for another Medical Board. I was still
categorised A2hBh and I returned to Binbrook to take up my duties. Our
task was to set up a unit with Lysanders that had been fitted out for target
towing, for bombers with trainee air gunners. The first Lysander was
delivered to us on 20 November, and I lost no time in having a dual
familiarisation flight. I had twenty minutes' dual instruction, and with an
improvement in the weather at the end of November I got several flights
on the 'Lizzies'. I enjoyed flying them, although they were so very
different from the lumbering Whitleys I had been used to. You had only

to have a good wind, and they would take off like a partridge breaking cover. I was surprised to find they were remarkably easy to handle – lots of power with a very short take-off and low landing speed. After being used to bombers, the handling technique was quite strange. Whereas the take-off on a Whitley required three-quarters of the length of the airfield before it became unstuck, the Lysander would get airborne in the length of a hangar. Stalling speed was about 45 knots, and in a high wind it was possible to take off in a few yards.

Nearly all the pilots on my unit were ex-operational aircrew and had been taken off operational duties for a 'rest' period. Some, like myself, were also restricted to limited flying for medical reasons. Flying Officer Edmunds had undergone extensive plastic surgery and under the skilled hands of Archibald McIndoe, at Stoke Mandeville Hospital, he had had his face restored to something more resembling a recognisable 'face'.

Ed, as we got to calling him, had fallen in love with one of his nurses and was engaged to be married on Saturday, 29 November. Our chaps decided to give him a proper bachelor party send-off. We met at the Ship Hotel in Grimsby and it was not long before poor old Ed was well and truly plastered. I said to Ed, 'Whatever is your wish in your last hour of bachelorhood, it shall be granted.' I must have been pretty plastered myself. But he managed a drunken stammer in reply: 'I wish a blonde!'

'You shall have a blonde!' I replied, looking around the hotel lounge. I noticed a naval officer, with a most beautiful blonde girl. I approached them and asked if they would do me a favour.

'My friend over there is getting married tomorrow and has expressed a last bachelor wish – to have a blonde. Would you feel like granting his wish?'

Without hesitation they both agreed. She came over to the table and sat on Ed's lap, put her arms around his neck and kissed him. It was an act of total selfless kindness. As a result of his burns, he had lost a lot of his hair, but he had trained some of it across the top of his forehead. As she kissed him she stroked her hand across his hair, and he muttered, as he slid slowly under the table, 'Ish shlovely, Ish shlovely!'

On 7 December 1941 the Japs declared war and on the 9th they sank the *Prince of Wales* and the *Repulse* off Malaya. We were shattered.

Slowly we were allocated a few Lysanders. Various items of equipment were delivered. Gradually we built up a 'circus', one Tiger Moth, six

Lysanders, four Whitleys and five Wellington ICs; later we acquired a Defiant. I was summoned to Group HQ at Eawtry, where I was given some sort of vague programme, but it was left very much to my own initiative, motivation and drive to get things organised. I really got very little help from Group.

The weather at this time of the year restricted our activities, so we did not get a lot of flying in during the winter months. Progress was very slow, but gradually we developed a semblance of a cohesive unit. I had to make frequent visits to No. 1 Group HQ, where no one seemed to be taking our unit seriously, and I had to make myself unpopular trying to get any dynamic action, and getting the bods at Group to pull their fingers out.

Our riggers carried out the modifications to the Lysanders to fit them out with target towing gear. A crew member would be detailed to operate the cable and drogue. The object was to fly along the Lincolnshire coast towing the drogue target while aircraft from the squadrons would come alongside and give their rear gunners the opportunity to carry out firing practice.

Our earliest attempts at target towing were not very successful. At least all the blokes, aircrew as well as ground crew, were dead keen, with enthusiasm as though they were on operational squadrons. We eventually got it right. The objective was to rendezvous with an aircraft from one of the squadrons from No. 1 Group, fly along together (it could not be called 'formation flying'), then stooge up and down the coast line with the gunner firing off trying to hit the drogue. Not as easy as it seemed. Then return to count the number of holes in the target. That was a piece of cake, until we had to liaise with the Polish squadrons. The posting to the TT & GT flight was to be a rest from the hazards and stress of operational flying. Some of the Poles had the idea that the target was the Lysander. One or two of our pilots applied for immediate posting back to an operational squadron: 'Far less dodgy.'

Life on 1481 flight had its good moments as well as the dicey ones. Returning from off Mablethorpe on one occasion I got caught out in a 'sea hard'. This is a local phenomenon, when a sea mist suddenly rolls inland without any warning. Visibility could have been perfect before, but in a matter of minutes down to a few hundred yards. We had no W/T and only R/T, so we could not get any homing bearings from base. I had no choice but to come down to tree-top level where I could see the ground.

I had got to know Lincolnshire like the back of my hand, so I had no difficulty identifying Louth. I was soon able to pick up the Louth Market Rasen road, and headed for Binbrook, following the road just above tree-top level. From Louth there is a road junction, which forks right to Binbrook, and from there I would have no difficulty in turning off to the aerodrome. No problem! By now visibility was so much worse that the seagulls were walking, but as long as I kept the road in sight I was quite happy. I do not think my drogue operator passenger was quite so confident. Reducing my speed as we approached the junction, I thought I was going too fast to take the corner, forgot for a moment I was flying and applied my hand brake! It sounds like a hell of a good 'line-shoot', but I did land safely at Binbrook.

The weather in December was dreadful most days but we did manage to get a few flights in during the month. I took fourteen days' leave to be with Marie over Christmas. This was a particularly welcome break as Marie was expecting our first child and was now seven months pregnant. She had decided to have her baby, which was due in the middle of February, at a maternity home in Southport. It was a very happy time for us, but I did not relish spending another three months away from her until she could come and join me again at Binbrook.

The weather turned more favourable during the first half of January, so we made the most of the opportunity to get in quite a lot of flying, but it deteriorated again during the latter part of the month. This gave us a chance to undertake some ground defence exercise and rifle practice. We all had to be prepared for a possible attack on the aerodrome by German parachutists. My unit was given the responsibility for defending a sector to the north of the aerodrome. Part of the training included preparation against a possible gas attack, so we all had to undergo a spell in a gas chamber, to get used to wearing gas masks in real gas conditions. There were also lectures on airfield defence, tanks and armoured units. It all seemed rather futile, as a handful of highly trained and disciplined German paratroops would have made mincemeat of us.

What was to have been the British equivalent to the French Resistance was the Local Defence Volunteer (LDV) Force, later to become the Home Guard, and defence of the aerodrome was one of their tasks. From time to time there was be an exercise to test the capabilities of the LDV. Local Army units would be detailed to 'attack' the aerodrome. To back up the LDV, which was a little thin on the ground, RAF personnel were given the task of supporting them – or was it the other way round? The RAF regiment was also somewhat under strength. So RAF personnel who were not required for operational duties were detailed to defend a sector of the airfield.

Having been put through the rudiments of aerodrome defence, it was decided that we should put our new skills to the test. Although we had had weapons training with Smith & Wesson revolvers, and Lee-Enfield rifles, we were certainly not trained for ground combat duties. What good we would have been against a highly trained enemy is anybody's guess. However, the order was given that an exercise would take place and that No. 1481 Target Towing and Gunnery Training flight personnel would 'defend' the northern sector of the airfield. We were issued with blank ammunition and 'grenade' bangers. The local detachment of the Army would 'attack' the aerodrome.

Everything would have gone along just fine, if the 'brown jobs' had played the game. They just would not lie down when they had been 'shot', and there were not enough umpires to ensure that everyone played fair. The Army was closing in on our dispersal units and things began to get a bit nasty. Our courageous TT & GT boys took their responsibilities very seriously and were determined to defend their dispersal unit to the last man. As gunshots and bangers did not deter the 'enemy', when they eventually closed in our gallant lads resorted to unarmed combat! I recall seeing an 'attacking' soldier, who obviously had not realised he had been spotted, creeping up behind a hedge. Although I had fired off all my 'shots' at almost point-blank range, he still came on. Nevertheless a good time was had by all, but we never did forgive the 'Pongos'. One shudders to think what the result might have been if there had been a real attack from German paratroops!

January had been intensely cold, and temperatures as low as 16 degrees Fahrenheit had been recorded. All the same, we did manage to get in quite a lot of flying. February brought heavy falls of snow and a complete stand-down from flying.

With our baby expected in mid-February, I took a forty-eight-hour pass to go and see Marie. She was pretty big and I would not have been surprised if the baby had come then. However, she was in very good health, so I returned to Binbrook, with a little more peace of mind. The weather was still terrible, with heavy falls of snow, and, with no equipment for snow clearing, everything came to a standstill. The break gave me another chance to get some more defence training, with lectures on tanks and armoured divisions.

On 17 February I received the news that I had been waiting for. A baby girl was born at half-past midnight. I took a Lysander and flew to Woodvale aerodrome, and took Sergeant Starr with me to fly the plane back. The cloud was 10/10ths all the way, so I flew above cloud and came down on ETA right on the coast, within half a mile of the aerodrome. I went straight to the nursing home, found mother and daughter doing fine. I spent seven days' leave with Marie and Anne and returned to Binbrook by train. It just happened that Sergeant Starr lived near Woodvale, and as the weather was too bad for him to return to Binbrook immediately he had a couple of days with his family.

The bad weather persisted, with heavy snow followed by several days of fog. Towards the middle of March we had our first Whitley V delivered to us – the intention being to have air gunners attached to us from squadrons, so that their operational aircraft would not have to be used for these training flights. Altogether we had four Whitleys delivered to us and then later we received five Wellington ICs. We now had a real 'flying circus'. From then on I flew the Whitleys and only occasionally took up a Lizzie. I still found more satisfaction flying the Whitley, even though the Lizzie was easy to fly.

On 22 March I had to attend another board at Halton. The result was the same, still A2hBh. After that there was a marked improvement in the weather in April. Although I was still restricted to a maximum height of 5,000 feet, I took a Whitley up to 12,000 feet one day to find out if I could cope. There were no ill effects, so I regarded the result of the board with some scepticism.

I was now getting anxious to have Marie and the baby come to live with me, as soon as possible. Whatever time I could get off duty, I would go house hunting, but the response was always the same; as soon as I mentioned we had a baby they did not want to know. By mid-May I discovered an absolutely delightful cottage in a romantic setting with roses round the door, about 6 miles from the aerodrome, at a village called Valesby. The cottage was owned by a farmer's wife who charged us only a nominal rent. At the end of May I drove to Southport and returned with Marie and the baby. We moved in on 30 May. The farmer's wife was a very kind and generous lady, and frequently my wife found vegetables, eggs and milk, which she had left on the doorstep and would not accept any money for them.

By then the weather had improved and day after day the weather was glorious. From then on we enjoyed a really hot spell. Suddenly life was very rosy; to be together again, in this lovely cottage, with glorious weather. It seemed like heaven, and the war seemed a million miles away.

Early in 1942 there was a marked change in the direction of the Royal Air Force's bomber offensive. A new directive was issued and a new commander appointed, of whom there will be more below. RAF Bomber Command, under Air Chief Marshal Sir Arthur Harris, was out to prove its worth, and in May 1942 the city of Cologne became the target for the first of the unprecedented 1,000-bomber raids. Further large-scale attacks followed. Harris's front-line bomber squadrons simply did not have the numbers of aircraft available to enact this statement of war-winning potential. He looked to his training units to muster the necessary strength.

From the beginning of May we had become aware that something big was on. On the night of 30 May, the first 1,000-bomber raid was launched on Cologne. Again on 1 June another 1,000 bombers attacked Essen.[2]

I was summoned to Groupy's office and was informed that all my unit's bombers were to be brought up to operational serviceability. So this was what the flap was all about. Every aircraft that could carry bombs was to be made operational to join in the attacks. All of them had previously been Category 'C', which meant they had been involved in some accident or damage that made them unfit for operational flying! Now they were to be brought up to Category 'A' – four clapped-out Whitleys and five Wellington ICs. Additional ground staff were attached to my unit and experienced aircrews were also attached to us, until we had a full strength of nine complete aircrews, and the ground staff to service the aircraft. We knew then what we were in for. We air-tested again and again, did night-flying circuits and bumps, and cross-country flights. All the aircraft had to have the compasses swung and all armaments thoroughly checked and test fired.

While all of this was going on, those of our aircrew who had had operational experience, and were fit for operational flying, were put on intensive refresher training. I spent much of my time taking other pilots under dual instruction, or as second pilot for experience of cross-country flights. While I assumed the role of the instructor, I left the flying of the Lizzies to those pilots who had not had experience on bombers. I was in my element again, as I much preferred to fly my first love, Whitleys.

One warm sunny evening in mid-June, our officers were invited to the Sergeants' Mess for drinks. The evening was strictly formal, and after a few quick drinks we left, while the evening was still light. I had parked my car at the rear of the Sergeants' Mess. When I went to get it, I found a group of about half a dozen 'bods' around my car, evidently up to no good.

'Someone has pissed in your tank!' I was warned. There was not much I could do about it, so I replied, 'Well, it was probably 70 per cent alcohol anyway, so it should not matter.' I pressed the starter button, and much to everyone's amazement the engine sprang to life immediately. The chaps just stood and gaped as I drove off.

The follow Saturday I had arranged to take Marie to Grimsby for the afternoon. We had just passed the camp entrance, when the engine cut out, although the gauge still showed the tank was still nearly a quarter full. Realising what had happened, I had to remove the pipe to the carburettor and drain off the 'offending fluid'. The fuel system on the baby Austin comprised a two-way cock, with a pipe sticking up to the tank. In normal use the cock would be set to draw off petrol from the top of the pipe. When the level of petrol went below the top of the pipe, the cock would be switched over to draw from the bottom of the tank. This provided one gallon as 'reserve'. As petrol floats on 'water', while the level of fuel was above the stack pipe, petrol would be drawn off, but as soon as I switched over to the reserve, it would be drawing off brine!

From May to July I was getting in quite a lot of flying, including night flying. Unfortunately, as I was still Category A2hBh (medically unfit for operational flying), I could not take part in the next raid. I just had to watch my chaps go off without me. All nine got off and all nine got back, although not all of them had got to the target. Some had had to turn back with engine trouble or some other problem. I made up my mind then that next time I would jolly well go with them. I had a word with the Group Medical Officer, and got him to arrange a Medical Board for me as soon as possible. I attended the board on 10 July and was passed fit for operational duties – home service only. That was good enough for me. I had already been getting in quite a lot of hours on daylight cross-countries and on the 28th I was told our unit would be on the next raid. This time I would be included. I did a three-hour cross-country and stood by every day doing air tests, until we got the word, 'We're on tonight chaps!'

I was full of self-confidence, and had a great sense of pride that I would be taking part with 1481 flight in the next 1,000-bomber raid.

Richard clearly was not aware at the time that this was not actually going to be a literal '1,000-bomber' raid, although it was going to involve 630 aircraft and the training units would indeed be called upon to raise the bomb tonnage that could be delivered. On the night of 31 July–1 August 1942 RAF Bomber Command despatched 308 Wellingtons, 113 Lancasters, 70 Halifaxes, 61 Stirlings, 54 Hampdens and 24 Whitleys, the latter consisting of the Whitleys of 1481 flight. By the end of the night parts of Düsseldorf lay in ruins and Bomber Command recorded 29 aircraft and crews lost. Richard Pinkham and his crew could count themselves lucky that they had not been part of the loss statistics.

Our kites took off an hour before the rest of the squadrons. Their aircraft were so much faster. I had a crew of experienced operational chaps. They all knew their stuff very well, and I was more than happy to have them all with me. We checked and double-checked everything. We took the Whitley that I had flown quite a lot, so we were all completely at ease, both with the aircraft and with ourselves. We taxied out for take-off, got a 'green' from the aerodrome control pilot, and were soon lumbering towards evening dusk, watching the glim lights of the flare path flashing past. The Merlin engines were running as smoothly as a sewing machine – the sound was music to my ears. I had been used to flying the old Whitleys without a load, and now we had a full load of bombs and fuel, so it seemed ages before we became unstuck. I was very relieved when we ceased bumping along the ground and felt the smoothness of becoming airborne.

It was a glorious evening, as we set course for Orford Ness, climbing steadily. It was just like old times, which was strange at first, but we soon settled down to standard cockpit drill. Wheels 'up', flaps 'up', pitch 'coarse', throttle back to 'climbing' boost. Check all instruments, set compass 140 degrees. We passed Orford Ness and joined the main stream of traffic, astonished to see dozens of other aircraft flying in the same direction and height. The sky seemed full of them. I had never seen so many aircraft in the sky at the same time. It was an astounding sight. The thought passed through my mind, 'God, we're going to give Jerry hell tonight!' The target was Düsseldorf, a trip that would normally have been expected to take about seven to eight hours.

Once we were well over the North Sea at about 10,000 feet, I told the rear gunner to test his guns and turret. He fired off a few rounds and traversed his turret through 180 degrees, and reported everything to be in good working order. He continued to traverse his turret, keeping a sharp look-out for fighters, as well as for any of our own aircraft, which might have been getting too close. There were so many, there was always a serious risk of collision. We were approaching the Dutch coast, when the rear gunner called out that he was having difficulty getting the turret to traverse more than 30 degrees each way.

'Not to worry,' I said. 'I'm quite sure you can fix it.'

'Sure skipper.' He sounded full of confidence.

After about ten minutes he called me again on the intercom.

'It's still not any better skip.'

'Never mind,' I replied. 'We probably won't need them.'

And so we carried on. We were right over Holland, but surprisingly there was only very slight flak, but intense searchlight activity. I thought, 'That's ominous, and a sure indication for night fighters.' The searchlights would give the position, direction and height of our chaps. This would bring the fighters onto our track. Then, as the searchlights caught a bomber, the fighters would pounce. It was not long before this is just what happened. We saw one of our aircraft caught in the searchlights, and the next thing we saw was him going down in flames. We were too far away to see if it was a fighter, but presumed it must have been, as there was no flak. Neither could we see if any parachutes had opened. Then a few moments later we saw another go down. There could be no doubt that fighters were in the area. It is one thing to be able to ward off an attack if your guns are useable, but, if your turret is u/s, it is like a boxer in the ring with his hands tied behind his back. You cannot hit back.

'Does anyone feel brave enough to press on, with a duff turret?' There was no reply. When we got back to base we found we had a bad leak in the turret hydraulics.

The episode was recorded in verse.

Written in the Honour and Glory of 1481 flight, concerning one particular episode in its not altogether blameless career. July 1942:

There was once a flap, well a kind of a flap.
But really it was only a trap,
To stop us from quaffing too much of the ale,
That down at the 'Marquis' is sometimes on sale.

If you listen, I'll tell you without delay,
How it happened, 'twas just this way.
I hope you'll believe me. It's doubtful I know.
But nevertheless spare a moment or so.

Well Harris rang Group, and Groupy rang us,
Saying, 'Look here, chaps, here's a deuce of a fuss.
Can you dig out a Whitley, or perhaps three or four,
And dash off and bomb the jolly old Ruhr?'

Twas 'Pinkie' who answered, and scratching his head,
Saying 'I'm afraid the poor old Whitleys are dead.
But we'll bring them to life, if you give us a start.
Go on there old chap do have a heart.'

While Groupy considered our 'Edie' came in,
And stood in amazement, as the sound of the din,
Of 'Pinkie' and Groupy, both thinking aloud,
And horrified shouts of the rest of the crowd.

He said, 'What's all the fuss' and 'Can I go home?'
While 'Pinkie' excitedly yelled on the phone.
'I've got just the man, provided of course,
We give him a pilot and crew that reads Morse.'

So it was agreed, that the Whitleys should go,
With a start of a quarter of an hour or so.
Thought Groupy, 'Why worry, they're so jolly fast,
I could give them a day, and they'd still be the last.'

So 'Jock' tuned the Whitleys, and did a fine job,
Though they're still not worth more than a couple of bob.
And for nearly a week, we did NFT's.
'We'll make it,' we thought, 'though we'll be on our knees.'

By day we were briefed, and by night we stood by,
Just sat in the Whitleys, just waiting to fly.
One night I sat in three feet of water.
While the rest were content, with just two and a quarter.

Yes, for days we were briefed, and when this was done,
We made preparations to hammer the Hun.
And at last we were airborne, or perhaps I should say,
We got off the ground, to join in the fray.

And much has been said, and there's still more to say,
Concerning cross-countries to Mablethorpe Bay.
But here I assure you, whatever our plight,
We at least put our hearts in the effort that night.

Of the three that were airborne, two crossed the Dutch coast,
And though they turned back, that's no idle boast.
The third did its best, but couldn't gain height,
And had to turn back, with the coast just in sight.

Now to this sad tale, a postscript I'll add,
Concerning one 'Harrison', a somewhat bright lad,
Who though rather fond of the aircraft he flew,
Was shortly to leave it and therefore felt blue.

So bringing it down, from some eight thousand feet,
He circled the 'drome and thought, 'What a treat.
I'll write the thing off, while Groupy's not there,
And when he gets back, that'll get in his hair.'

So he made his approach, and crashed it with ease,
Now there's 'M' for Mother, alone on her knees.
Now he's posted to 'Twelve', and I chuckle with glee,
To think what he'll do to a Wellington Three!

A fortnight later, I was posted to No. 150 Squadron at Snaith, for another tour of ops. I had very little warning, and Marie and the baby had to return to Southport by train, but I was granted a forty-hours pass at the weekend, before reporting for duty on Monday, 24 August.

I had completely recovered from whatever it was that had ailed me; the 'rest' period had been a welcome break from the pressure of intensive flying as a pilot for aircrew under training at Abingdon.

I would now be able to prove to the chief flying instructor at Abingdon that I was certainly NOT LMF.

6. Once More unto the Breach

In the year and a half since Richard had been part of a Bomber Command operational squadron the RAF's heavy bomber force had been subject to substantial growth and development. The weight of explosive that could be released on a target was substantially greater, many more aircraft could be sent on individual raids and the bomber aircraft were able to carry considerably more ordnance than in the early days of the war. The introduction into operations of the four-engine heavy bombers, the Short Stirling (February 1941), Handley Page Halifax (March 1941) and Avro Lancaster (March 1942), were instrumental in this escalation, although many squadrons still operated with some of the stalwarts, such as the Wellington.

At a strategic level a succession of policy changes had shifted Bomber Command's priorities from attacking oil, to aiding the Navy, which was struggling to keep the Atlantic supply routes flowing. Then a directive of 9 July 1941 requested an escalation of attacks on the German transportation system and to destroy 'the morale of the civil population as a whole and of the industrial workers in particular'.[1] But the belief in the capabilities of the bomber offensive received a serious setback when the Butt Report was published in August 1941. An analysis of just over 4,000 photographs, taken by aircraft attacking targets between June and July 1941, revealed some startling statistics. For example, only one in four of the crews that reported bombing a target was found to be within 5 miles of the respective target. In the full-moon period it was a marginally better strike rate, but in the non-moon periods it was markedly worse; only one in fifteen crews managed to bomb within 5 miles. On top of this it was also reported that only two-thirds of the crews sent on a raid had even found the target. Through the winter months of late 1941 and early 1942 Bomber Command's future came under the closest scrutiny; was it worth such an investment of resources. Those who argued for a development, continuation and escalation of the bomber offensive would eventually win through. February 1942 was quite a turning point for Bomber Command. Air Chief Marshal Sir Arthur Harris took over command of the RAF's heavies with the responsibility to implement a new directive issued just over a week before he was appointed. 'It has been decided that the primary objective of your operations should now be focused on the morale of the enemy civil population and in particular of the industrial workers.'[2] Harris was convinced of the war-winning potential of the bomber and he had no qualms about unleashing the blunt weaponry of the bomber against Germany. It is reported that when he witnessed the Luftwaffe bombing of London earlier in the war he commented that the Germans, having 'sown the wind', would 'reap the whirlwind'.

To implement this new focus, changes had also taken place at a tactical level. The days of the lone bomber were long gone. Bomber Command aircraft would penetrate enemy air space en masse, attempting to swamp defences, with various changes of direction en route to and from the target, attempting to deceive the controllers of the German night-fighter aircraft, who had seen an escalation in the resources that they could call on. The numbers of twin-engine Messerschmitt 110s and Junkers 88s designated for night duties had risen accordingly, as had the numbers of flak guns, searchlights and personnel to man the weaponry. The battle in the night skies over Germany in 1942 was markedly different from that in 1940. The German night-fighter threat was considerably more potent.

Sir Arthur Harris had been quick to demonstrate the potential of his bomber force. Devastating attacks on Lübeck and Rostock in March and April 1942 respectively had given cause for optimism, and the mustering of resources to mount the 1,000-bomber raids in May and June demonstrated what could be achieved. In addition, by August 1942, the fledgling Pathfinder Force was ready to operate. Established to locate, identify and mark targets for the 'main force', the Pathfinders certainly experienced teething troubles, but they would eventually prove themselves. When Richard Pinkham returned to start his second tour with an operational squadron in August 1942, the spinning vortices of Sir Arthur Harris's 'whirlwind' were combining and gathering pace.

No. 150 Squadron, RAF Snaith

The immediate impression on arriving at Snaith is that one has been posted to the Middle East. In fact the aerodrome and surrounding countryside are bleak and barren. The illusion is further accentuated following a hot, dry summer, when everywhere is arid and dusty. Not surprisingly it acquired the nickname 'Benghazi'. I arrived on 24 August 1942.

The squadron was equipped with Wellington Mark IIIs, and, although I had taken the opportunity to get as much time as possible on Wimpey ICs while at Binbrook, I had not yet had a bash on the Mark IIIs, which were powered with much more powerful Hercules X engines. The difference in power was most exhilarating. They were beautiful engines, and, although there had been trouble in the early days with these power units, the problem had been overcome, and I never had any trouble with them myself.

No sooner had I booked in with the station adjutant than I was conducted forthwith to the squadron offices, where I was introduced to Flight Lieutenant J. W. Kirwan, who was acting flight commander 'B' flight. Shortly afterwards he was promoted to Squadron Leader. I did at least have time to get down to the Mess, where I was allocated a room and dumped my kit. Next morning I reported to the flight commander, when I was detailed to go up with Sergeant Homer for twenty minutes' 'experience on type'. After flying Whitleys and Wimpey ICs, I found that the Hercules engines were a real thrill.

The urgency with which I had been posted to the squadron, and sent up straight away the next morning, was some indication how much the bombing effort was being stepped up. I got a few hours' familiarisation on a Wimpey III, and getting to know my new crew. Two nights later we did some local flying and on the 28th we were on the battle orders for a raid on Saarbrücken.

On the night of 28–9 August 1942 No. 150 Squadron contributed 11 aircraft to the 113 sent to Saarbrücken. Two Wellingtons would be forced to abandon the raid, owing to technical problems. The remaining No. 150 Squadron bombers attacked the target and on the return journey one crew had to endure the attention of a night-fighter, the Squadron ORB recording 'eight combats taking place before the engagement ended, our aircraft received a number of hits'. On return to friendly skies, two aircraft were diverted to Elsham and three others, including that in which Richard Pinkham was flying, had to land at other aerodromes owing to fuel shortage. One of the squadron's Wellingtons was written off at Middle Wallop without injury to the crew, following a crash-landing, when some incendiaries caught fire and the aircraft was engulfed by flames.

On 28 August 1942 I was detailed to fly to Saarbrücken as second dickie to Flight Lieutenant Kirwan. No sooner had we crossed the Belgian coast than the flak was concentrated on us. We may have been off course and out of the mainstream of bombers. The flak was not very accurate and we treated it with some disdain, until suddenly there was an enormous burst dead ahead, like a giant chandelier! In fact it was like a typical firework burst of hundreds of star lights. The sudden and unexpected cascade of stars directly ahead of us gave me a bit of a fright. It seemed very close and we soon flew right through the middle of the 'chandelier', but nothing hit us.

The weather was very dodgy, and, although we located the target, we could not be certain that we had hit the target. Although Saarbrücken was about 250 miles inland, most of the route was clear of defences, but we did receive a lot of attention from heavy flak over the target area.

The Wellington IIIs did not have anything like the range of the Whitley, but, as our cruising speed was 160 knots, and we usually cruised at 15,000 feet, it only took us about an hour and half from crossing the Belgian coast. The return flight was uneventful, but we were diverted to RAF Bassingbourn for refuelling.

Ours was the only aircraft to be diverted to Bassingbourn that night, and consequently we received personal attention. From the moment we landed we were whisked off for debriefing, where we were offered a choice of hot beverages or soup, and informed that breakfast was waiting for us in the Mess. All this VIP treatment had been laid on solely for our benefit.

We arrived at the Mess at about three o'clock, where we were greeted by two gorgeous WAAF orderlies, waiting to attend on our every need. (At least that is what they told us!) Lashings of bacon, eggs and baked beans were ready for us. The two WAAFs were most charming and attentive. The thought passed through my mind, 'This all makes ops worthwhile!' We felt we were in seventh heaven.

'Was there anything else you would like sir?'

'Depends what you have got to offer,' I replied.

'Would you like us to put on some music?'

'Sounds a good idea. Yes please.'

'Would you like a beer?'

'Would I just – but surely the bar is closed.'

'Leave it to us,' they replied, and produced five pints!

'Now is there anything else you would like?'

'Such as…?'

'What about a dance? Or are you too tired?'

Squadron Leader Richard Pinkham DFC, September 1944, when serving with the 3rd Tactical Air Force, Comilla, Bengal. *(Richard Pinkham)*

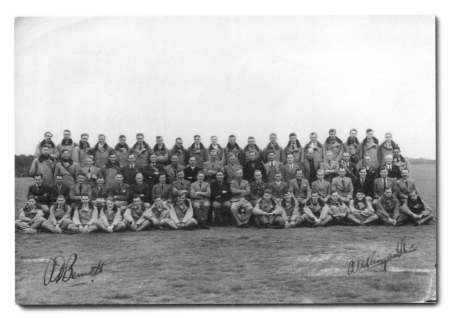

Elementary Flying Training School, Gatwick and Fairoaks. Richard sitting in the front row, third from the left. *(Richard Pinkham)*

Fairoaks 1939.
Gas masks on.
(Richard Pinkham)

Raw recruits at Guildford station awaiting a train to Gatwick. Richard Pinkham fifth from the left. *(Richard Pinkham)*

Tiger Moth at Fairoaks in September 1939. *(Richard Pinkham)*

Richard in the front seat of a Miles Magister at Gatwick. *(Richard Pinkham)*

Officers' Mess, South Cerney, November 1939, No. 3 Flying Training School. *(Richard Pinkham)*

Richard at No. 3 Flying Training School, South Cerney, December 1939. *(Richard Pinkham)*

Snaps taken on Richard's travels. Clockwise from top: Miles Master; Miles Master from a different angle; Hawker Hart; Airspeed Oxford. *(Richard Pinkham)*

More of Richard's snaps. Clockwise from top: Fairey Battle; Boulton Paul Defiant; Bristol Beaufort; Bristol Blenheim. *(Richard Pinkham)*

Richard Pinkham standing third from the right at No. 77 Squadron. *(Richard Pinkham)*

Official photograph of one of the first Whitley Mk Vs that went into service with No.77 Squadron in September 1939. The following year Richard Pinkham would be flying such an aircraft into battle. *(IWM ATP 9616B)*

Richard's 'office'. Here an unknown sergeant is at the controls of an Armstrong Whitworth Whitley of No. 10 Operational Training Unit, Abingdon, Berkshire. July 1940. *(IWM CH 700)*

No. 77 Squadron's Whitley V, KN–O *(Richard Pinkham)*

German invasion barges waiting at Boulogne Harbour, France during the Battle of Britain. June 1940. *(IWM MH 6657)*

YEAR		AIRCRAFT		PILOT, OR 1ST PILOT	2ND PILOT, PUPIL OR PASSENGER	DUTY (INCLUDING RESULTS AND REM
		Type	No.			
—		—	—		—	TOTALS BROUGHT FOR
Nov	12	WHITLEY V	T4226	SELF	CREW	CRA 701 WESELING SUCCESSFUL
	14	WHITLEY V	T4169	SELF	CREW	AIR TEST
	14	WHITLEY V	T4169	SELF, S/L HOWARD	CREW	FAR585 BERLIN SUCCESSFU
	16	WHITLEY V	T4169	SELF	CREW	PTB131 HAMBURG SUCCESSFU

S/L Howard s/L.

O C "A Flight. No. 77

Summary for NOVEMBER 19 40   1. _____
Unit "77" 77" Sqn. Aircraft   2. WHITLEY V
Date 2·12·40   3. _____
Signature Richard M Pinkham   4. _____
770

DEC	3	WHITLEY V	T4226	SELF	CREW	BXC MANNHEIM TARGET LO
	7	WHITLEY V	T4279	SELF	CREW	LOCAL FLYING, AIR TEST
	10	WHITLEY V	T4279	SELF	CREW	WEST FREUGH X-COUNTRY
	10	WHITLEY V	T4279	SELF	CREW	CRS361 MANNHEIM BAD WE
	12	WHITLEY V	T4279	SELF	CREW	AIR TEST
	12	WHITLEY V	T4279	SELF	CREW	RECALLED OWING TO FOG
	15	WHITLEY V	T4279	SELF	CREW	BXC126 MADGEBURG SUCCESSF
	16	WHITLEY V	P4967	SELF	CREW	TO YEADON
	16	WHITLEY V	P4938	SELF	CREW	YEADON - BASE
	20	WHITLEY V	P4938	SELF	CREW	FLYING TEST
	21	WHITLEY V	P4938	SELF	CREW	CNY669 MERSEBURG TARGET NOT L LAND AT YEAD
	21	WHITLEY V	P4938	SELF	CREW	YEADON - BASE
	23	WHITLEY V	T4279	SELF	CREW	AIR TEST, CONSUMPTION TEST, GEORGE

GRAND TOTAL [Cols. (1) to (10)]
482 Hrs. 45 Mins.   TOTALS CARRIED FORWA

Richard Pinkham's logbook, November/December 1940. *(Richard Pinkham)*

SINGLE-ENGINE AIRCRAFT				MULTI-ENGINE AIRCRAFT						PASS-ENGER	INSTR./CLOUD FLYING (Incl. in cols. (1) to (10))	
DAY		NIGHT		DAY			NIGHT					
Dual	Pilot	Dual	Pilot	Dual	1st Pilot	2nd Pilot	Dual	1st Pilot	2nd Pilot		Dual	Pilot
(1)	(2)	(3)	(4)	(5)	(6)	(7)	(8)	(9)	(10)	(11)	(12)	(13)
33·20	35·35			32·00	120·45	14·20	8·00	160·45	4·00	21·10	13·50	60·55
								7·30				7·30
					·30							
								9·10				9·10
								9·40				9·40
					4·25			44·45				
								10·15				10·15
					1·30							
					2·00							
								8·00				8·00
					·45							
								1·20				1·20
								10·10				10·10
					·30							
					·15							
					2·00							·30
								9·00				9·00
					·15							
					1·10							
33·20	35·35			32·00	129·40	14·20	8·00	225·50	4·00	21·10	13·50	126·30
(1)	(2)	(3)	(4)	(5)	(6)	(7)	(8)	(9)	(10)	(11)	(12)	(13)

Avro Anson flying from Abingdon, May 1941. *(Richard Pinkham)*

Blida town and airfield at the base of the Atlas mountains. *(Richard Pinkham)*

Richard's snap of 'The Rock, Gibraltar', December 1942. *(Richard Pinkham)*

5 March 1943. Vickers Wellington B Mark IIIs of No. 150 Squadron RAF are prepared for a night raid on Bizerta, at Blida, Algeria. In the foreground, armourers, stripped to the waist, wheel a trolley-load of 500-lb GP bombs towards an aircraft undergoing a final engine inspection. In the background, HF676 'JN-R' appears to be ready for action. *(IWM CNA 003970)*

Blida, 1943. Richard Pinkham just left of centre with the cap on. *(Richard Pinkham)*

Year		Aircraft		Pilot, or 1st Pilot	2nd Pilot, Pupil or Passenger	Duty (Including Results and Remarks)
Month	Date	Type	No.			
—	—	—	—	—	—	—
						Totals Brought Forward
Sept	7	Wellington III	X3885	Self	Crew	Night Flying Test
	8	Wellington III	X3805	Self	Crew	Night Flying Test
	8	Wellington III	X3805	Self	Crew	Operations on Frankfurt. Success. Emergency landing at Manston
	10	Wellington III	X3805	Self	Crew	Manston to Base. Low Level X-Cou
	10	Wellington III	X3805	Self	Crew	Operations on Dusseldorf. Success
	12	Wellington III	X3805	Self	Crew	Air Test Land at Binbrook
	13	Wellington III	X3805	Self	Crew	Air to Air Firing
	14	Wellington III	X3805	Self	Crew	Operations on Bremen. Success. Land at Binbrook
	14	Wellington III	X3805	Self	Crew	Binbrook to Base
	15	Wellington III	X3805	Self	Crew	Low Level Cross Country
	15	Wellington III	X3805	Self	Crew	Search Light & Fighter Co-op. Cross Cou
	16	Wellington III	X3805	Self	Crew	Air Test
	16	Wellington III	X3805	Self	Crew	Operations on Essen. Success. Land at Marham
	17	Wellington III	X3805	Self	Crew	Marham to Base
	18	Wellington III	X3805	Self	Crew	Mine Laying off Lorient. Success
	19	Wellington III	X3805	Self	Crew	Operations on Saarbrücken. Thre Loc
	21	Wellington III	X3805	Self	Crew	Low Level Cross Country, B/A Practi
	25	Oxford	DF413	P/O Swain	Self	B/A Instruction Figure 8 & Appr
	25	Oxford	415	P/O Swain	Self	B/A Instruction, Q.D.M & Approaches
	26	Oxford	DF413	P/O Swain	Self	B/A Instruction Q.D.M & Approach
	27	Oxford	413	P/O Swain	Self	B/A Instruction
	27	Oxford	413	P/O Swain	Self	B/A Instruction
	28	Oxford	413	P/O Swain	Self	B/A Practice

Grand Total [Cols. (1) to (10)]
832 Hrs. 40 Mins.

Totals Carried Forward

Richard Pinkham's logbook, September 1942, whilst with No. 150 Squadron in the UK.
(Richard Pinkham)

4 . 22-23 1.41. BIZERTA. S/L. PINKHAM. NT. F/8. 7000' 4. → X.   P. 15050DN.   B.

Bombs falling from Squadron Leader Richard Pinkham's Wellington onto Bizerta docks, Tunisia, 23 February 1943. *(Richard Pinkham)*

Officers of No. 150 Squadron at Blida, March 1943. Richard standing third from the left. *(Richard Pinkham)*

'Me, tired? Just let me show you!'

So we danced for an hour or so until daybreak. The flight had taken six hours and I had been flying the night before and air-tested the aircraft. So we had been on the go for over twenty-four hours without sleep, and here we were dancing, still in our flying boots. I felt great. But the dream had to end, and sadly we never saw the girls again. They deserved a gong for 'services beyond the call of duty'.

For a whole week we were standing by, and for three days we did air-testing. Then on 8 September we were 'on' again, this time with me as captain. The target was Frankfurt, and we were to carry a 4,000lb 'Blockbuster'! Because we would be carrying maximum bomb load, we had a correspondingly reduced fuel load. Although Frankfurt was not such a great distance, it was stretching it a bit fine.

It was a clear night with good visibility and broken cloud, so finding the target should not have been too difficult. We had to stooge around to get a good pinpoint, and with a 4,000-pounder on board, we wanted to make sure we were spot on target. It was too precious to waste, so after about half an hour over the target area, when we were satisfied that we were on target, we let it go. With the sudden release of 4,000lb the aircraft seemed to bounce up. The effect on the handling of the aircraft was quite dramatic. The controls were so much lighter, the aircraft trim and attitude quite different. It was a big load off our minds.

We were well aware that we had used up a lot of fuel stooging around over the target area, but we felt happy that we were well within our endurance limits. However, I was beginning to get a bit anxious as we approached the Belgian coast, so I told the navigator to keep a close watch on the fuel gauges. From time to time he reported the fuel situation to me, and soon he informed me that we had barely half an hour's fuel left! This would certainly not have been enough to get back home, so I asked him to give me a course for the nearest airfield to make a precautionary landing. There was not much moon, but at 15,000 feet we got a good pinpoint as we crossed the coast. By that time, the navigator told me we were down to less than twenty minutes' fuel. There was nothing for it, but to send out a mayday signal to make an emergency landing.

Manston airfield in Kent was specially equipped to deal with such a situation. The landing strip was 3,000 yards long and 200 feet wide and ideal for aircraft to make a belly landing, for those that had been shot up and badly damaged, or with engine failure, or short of fuel.

The most helpful facility, however, was the searchlight 'homing' scheme. No sooner had they received our mayday signal than dozens of searchlights in Kent and Surrey simultaneously sprang into life, all pointing in the direction of Manston, and intersecting directly over the airfield – a most remarkable display, and a very welcome sight. All that was necessary was to aim for the intersection of all the lights and safety.

From about 15,000 feet over the coast we throttled back to make a gradual descent with minimum revs, to conserve what little fuel we had left. I hoped in this way to stretch the glide so as to avoid the necessity of ditching in the Channel. I hoped the descent could be so controlled that we would be able to make a direct landing – no circuit, and no possibility of risking having to go round again. There would be no second chance.

The searchlights created a canopy of light over the aerodrome, transforming the whole area as though it was daylight. We got a 'green' from the aerodrome control to land straight ahead. Immediately we touched down, the searchlights were extinguished, a necessary precaution in case of the possibility of Jerry intruders. Although there was a vast grassed area, the airfield was littered with crashed aircraft. The airfield itself was also quite undulating, which certainly did not make landing any easier. It was a bumpy landing, but we were safe and relieved. We continued to coast along to the end of the flare path, but before I turned them off both engines cut. We were right out of fuel; there was not even enough to taxy off the end of the flare path. St Christopher had been working overtime for us that night.

The night of 8–9 September 1942 was not a good one for No. 150 Squadron. Two aircraft failed to return to friendly skies. One fell to flak, with the crew taken captive. Another fell to the guns of a German night-fighter with a total loss of life. A third Wellington was forced down while preparing to land at Lympne airfield in Kent, owing to a lack of fuel, and two men lost their lives.[3]

One of the key tactical developments in the escalation of the bomber offensive was the introduction of the bomber stream. The days of lone sorties were over; Bomber Command would try and pierce the night-fighter zones en masse, and swamp the defences on the ground. Any crew finding themselves isolated from the bomber stream were most certainly out on the proverbial limb. And if they were over a target, all the guns and all the searchlights would focus their attention. On the night of 10–11 September 1942 Richard and his crew proved the point.

RAF Bomber Command despatched 479 bombers of various types to Düsseldorf that night, including aircraft provided by training units. Leading the raid were 'Pathfinders'. Established in August 1942, the Pathfinder Force was designated as a specialist target-marking force – to find and mark the target for the 'main force'. They would soon achieve Group status as No. 8 (Path Finder Force) Group. In the early days of 'Pathfinding' problems arose as new systems, tactics and techniques were exposed to the harsh realities of operations. Nevertheless, the Pathfinders would go on to distinguish themselves as the war progressed. On the night of 10–11 September the Pathfinders could claim successful marking at Düsseldorf and the main force inflicted widespread destruction. The No. 150 Squadron ORB records that 'bombs were dropped by our aircraft with good effect, as fires were visible from 100 miles away on return'. But there was a cost to Bomber Command and thirty-three aircraft would not be returning from the raid, including five aircraft from one particular operational training unit. There was quite an air battle raging over Germany that night and in the midst of it was Flight Lieutenant Richard Pinkham.

We returned to base the following day to find that we had already been detailed for another op, this time to Düsseldorf. This target was right in the heart of the Ruhr Valley – known as 'Happy Valley'. It was very heavily defended, and the whole region was bristling with guns. We had to run the gauntlet, wherever the target was in the Ruhr.

For some reason we got badly off course – probably a change of wind speed or directions from the Met forecast. But, although we had taken a tail-drift sight, the navigator had not made a sufficient correction, and consequently we found ourselves well south of the target area – right into a hornets' nest. As we had deviated from the mainstream, we were isolated, and so received the undivided attention of searchlights and flak. It was not long before we were caught in a searchlight, and scores of others immediately fastened on to us. There seemed to be no escape; we were trapped in a cone. Heavy shells were bursting all round us and getting too bloody close. The aircraft was being buffeted by the explosions. We could hear the shells bursting and smell the cordite. Taking full evasive action, weaving, turning and corkscrewing, we somehow managed to survive. The searchlights still held us tenaciously. I was throwing the Wimpey about like a fighter, something it had not been designed to do, but still she responded well. Constantly changing height, speed and direction did not give the gunners time to get our range; nevertheless they were still too close for comfort.

With dozens of searchlights fastened on to us, there was no escape. I was blinded by the intense light. All I could do was to keep my head down. The instruments were useless. The Giro compass had toppled, and other instruments were spinning madly, so I had no idea where we were going. The magnetic compass was spinning like a top. I was literally flying by the seat of my pants. At times the searchlights appeared to be coming through the top of the cockpit, which could have meant only one thing – we were upside down!

All the time the constant steep turns caused us to lose height, and by now I was totally disorientated. I thought if I could get down really low the searchlights would struggle to hold me. Also light flak would have difficulty in lowering their elevation. There was the risk of barrage balloons, but, as the aircraft was fitted with an explosive cable cutter, this was a risk I felt reasonably safe to take. As it was, we never saw any balloons.

The reflection of the searchlights in a river was an absolute godsend. It would give me a guide to find my way out, and as long as I could follow the course of the river I could maintain a constant direction, and at the same time continue to weave following the bends in the river. I soon recognised that it was in fact the river Rhine. I realised that, if I followed the course of the river south, I would eventually get clear of the heavily defended area. By now I had descended to less than 500 feet and was getting lower as I endeavoured to avoid the light flak. By now I was sweating like a pig and my mouth was dry, but still they had not got me.

Then, straight ahead of us, I could pick out the silhouette of a bridge. I could see a gun post on the top of the bridge, actually firing down at us. I recognised it as Hohenzollern Bridge and had to pull up to get over it. All the time both front and rear gunners were firing off at searchlights and gun posts. The river still reflected the searchlights and I continued to follow the course of the river. Eventually we got clear of the guns, and as soon as I felt safe to do so I started to climb again. We climbed back to 12,000 feet and headed north to Düsseldorf. We found the target, bombed it and beat a hasty retreat for home. We returned to base without any further excitement; we had had enough for one night.

We landed safely back at base, taxied over to our dispersal area, and got out to look around the aircraft. Sure enough there were several holes, where shell splinters had hit us, but they had not caused damage to any vital parts. But it had been a very near thing. The boys on the ground were not too pleased at the mess their kite was in. Fortunately the damage was largely superficial and very quickly it was all made good. I continued to fly the same aircraft on several more ops.

We were not allowed any time to relax, as three days later we were on standby again. This time the target was Bremen. We were credited with having hit the target – 'mission successful'. This was confirmed from the night photograph we had brought back with us – the camera was synchronised to take a picture of the target as we dropped our bombs. It could be estimated from the photograph exactly where the bombs would fall. Clever blokes these intelligence officers. At least it was no good coming back and 'shooting a line' that you had pranged the target if you had not got a photograph to prove it. On returning we were diverted to Binbrook, as visibility at Snaith was poor. But by morning ground mist had cleared and we returned to base.

Twenty-one aircraft and crews would be lost on the raid to Bremen, including a Wellington from No. 150 Squadron. Sergeant H. F. Grace of the Royal Australian Air Force died along with his entire crew. The cause of the loss was never established, and nothing was ever found, so the names of the five men were etched into the walls of the Runnymede Memorial.

The next day we were sent on a low-level cross-country flight. This seemed rather strange. I wondered what the chaps at Group were up to. What death or glory stunt were they planning for us? There must obviously be some reason for this unusual variation from our normal operational duties. Or did they just think we needed more training? Then the same night we were detailed for a night cross-country. The object of this exercise was to provide our own fighters with interception practice. We did not see anything of the fighters, but on the other hand it could well have been that our rear gunner did not see them, and it was he who needed the practice.

During the whole of that week we flew six nights, five of which were operational sorties. As the weather is usually very good during September, it was a matter of taking full advantage of the good conditions. Unfortunately early morning mists would necessitate getting off early, so that we would be back before the mist closed in; otherwise, as often happened, we would be diverted to a station free of fog.

I had done plenty of practice on the Link trainer on simulated Z-Z landings but had never had the need to carry out landings in fog, using the beam-approach and landing equipment. It was one thing doing it as a simulated exercise on the Link trainer, where if you made a cock-up it was only your pride that got hurt; with the real thing there would be no room for mistakes.

In *The Bomber Command War Diaries* Martin Middlebrook and Chris Everitt claim the raid of 16–17 September 1942 by 369 aircraft to Essen was 'probably the most successful attack on this difficult target'. But it came at a price, as thirty-nine aircraft did not return, a very high loss rate of 10.6 per cent. To swell the size of the attacking force, Bomber Command had called upon the training units to provide crews. By the end of the night 200 airmen had lost their lives; 77 of these had been flying training unit aircraft. This would be the last time that the training units would get the call to support the main force operations in strength.

One Wellington from No. 150 Squadron was part of the loss statistics. Flak had taken out the port engine of Sergeant Randle's bomber, and when the starboard engine began to falter the crew took to their parachutes. All would survive, the pilot and four others evading capture, the other being taken into enemy custody.[4]

So it was on 16 September that we hit Essen, and again we were credited with 'mission successful', with a photograph to prove it. There was the usual amount of heavy flak and searchlights, which we had come to expect from this area. There was always the danger of some pilots becoming too casual and indifferent about the defences. After a number of ops, it was all too easy to imagine that one was untouchable, and consequently to be rather less careful, and of course that was when many chaps 'bought it'! When you have had a number of relatively easy trips, you think there is nothing to it, and tend to become overconfident. Once again we were diverted, to Marham, because fog had closed in at Snaith. We never relished these occasions, unless we could return the same morning.

The mine-laying undertaken by Bomber Command is one of the least well-known campaigns carried out by the bomber force. Perhaps historians have sidelined this substantial effort, as quantifying the results is difficult; there may also be the perception that it was less dangerous than the attacks on

city targets. But dangerous it certainly was, and many lives were sacrificed
for the cause – hindering and harassing enemy shipping. Britain had
been at war for almost three years and the Atlantic convoys bringing vital
survival supplies were under attack. Merchant seamen and thousands of
tons of cargo lay at the bottom of the ocean. It was truly a fight for survival
and a fight to maintain the strength to continue waging war. Bomber
Command senior commanders may not have been particularly keen on
attacking German warships, U-boats and the respective manufacturing
bases and harbours, which included the Atlantic ports in France. But the
high strategists felt it was necessary, and Bomber Command received
instructions accordingly.

The next op was to be something different, mine-laying off Lorient
(18 September 1942). We needed some light on a mission such as this, so
as the moon was in its first quarter it was not a completely black night.
It turned out to be a relatively easy trip. Our track took us over the Brest
Peninsular, so we were only over land for a short while. With the surf
breaking on the shore, we were able to pick out the Brittany coast
without any difficulty. We turned out to sea to let down to 500 feet,
descending down to 300 feet as we approached the dropping zone,
offloaded our mine and beat it back home.

Group must have thought, 'That was too easy!' We were back before
midnight and got a good night's sleep. 'They won't be tired,' thought
Group. 'So they can do another one tonight!' So that night we were on
again. Saarbrücken again! En route out we crossed the coast between
Ostend and Dunkirk, at a point where the defences were light. There
was a lot of cloud about, so we had to climb to 13,000 feet to get above
it. The moon was low in the sky, so it was a fairly dark night. We could
not see the coast, but altered course on dead reckoning. Gradually the
sky seemed to be getting lighter, and I could not figure out why this
should be. There was not sufficient moon to make it that light, and there
were no searchlights at that time. I thought it was possible that it could
have been a concentration of searchlights in the distance. But I decided
that it could not be searchlights, as the sky above was light. I called up
the rest of the crew to ask if they could see where the light was coming
from. It was quite eerie, as the light seemed to be weaving about like
searchlights, not as in the usual beams, but more like a curtain of light.
This must be Jerry's new secret defence system, and any minute now a
fighter would pounce on us. It occurred to me that all the light was on

our port side, and that the southern sky was quite dark. I called out
to Paddy.

'For God's sake, Paddy, keep your eyes skinned for fighters!'

I told the wireless operator to go into the astrodome and keep a good
look out there.

The rear gunner called out, 'The lights keep weaving, but they can't
be searchlights!' I banked sharply to port to get a better look for myself,
then it suddenly dawned on me that I had seen the phenomenon once
before. It was the Aurora Borealis (the Northern Lights). Had we not had
more urgent business to attend to, we would have enjoyed sticking
around and admiring the beauty of the spectacle.

We continued on course, heading for the target, but, because there
was so much cloud, the defences kept quiet. We got to the target area on
ETA, but could not see the ground at all. Although we stooged around
for quite a long time, we could not find a break in the clouds. At least so
long as we remained there the Jerrys had to stay in their shelters.
Eventually I decided we had stayed around long enough and set course
for home. We were airborne for six hours fifty minutes, which was near
the limit of endurance of these aircraft.

One aircraft from No. 150 Squadron failed to return, the entire crew of five,
including the pilot, Sergeant Northey, losing their lives. They are interred at
Choloy cemetery in France.

A few days later I was sent on a beam-approach training course at RAF
Holme. Having completed the course satisfactorily, I was certified
competent on standard beam-approach procedure. A week later I was
promoted to acting Squadron Leader, OC 'B' flight, with effect from
7 October.

We stood by for two days doing air tests. Eventually on 10 October we
were briefed for another mine-laying mission, off Saint-Nazaire. There
was not much moon now, but it was easy to pick out the coastline of the
Cherbourg Peninsular, identify Jersey and start descending across
Brittany. We had to come down to 500 feet as we approached the target,
and when we got a good pinpoint on the coast just north of the target we
turned out to sea and came down to 200 feet to make our run into the
dropping zone. There was some desultory flak but nothing to get excited
about. We watched the tracer shells approaching us (like a train coming
in the distance) and avoided them by climbing or diving slightly. The trip

took six and three-quarter hours, but, although we did not need to divert to a nearer airfield, we did not have much fuel reserve. As it was, there was no problem with visibility or the weather.

It was customary for the CO to go on ops from time to time. One day he was due to take one of the aircraft for an air test and for some reason he endeavoured to indicate something to the ground crew, opened the side window of the cockpit, and, putting his hand out to point something to one of the airmen, stuck his fingers into the arc of the propeller, which promptly sliced off his fingertips. He was lucky it was not his hand, but he was, of course, grounded, and shortly after Wing Commander Barclay was posted to the squadron as CO.

An anti-cyclone had settled over the British Isles, which gave us beautiful autumn days, but at the same time mist and fog descended usually after midnight, considerably restricting operational night flying. This enabled us to get in some much needed practice flying, such as single-engine flying and landing, beam approach and photography. Nearly a fortnight passed like this until the Met Officer told us that mist would not close in until early morning. So we were briefed for an early take-off. There was nearly a full moon and a clear sky. It looked like being an enjoyable flight.

I was first to get airborne, but we had been in the air for only fifty minutes when we got a recall signal. The Met Officer had made a bad boob with the forecast. Visibility had already started to deteriorate. Being first off I had got farthest by the time we received the signal and consequently I would be the last to get back to the airfield. While we were still some considerable distance from base, the glow of the paraffin flares could be seen through the thick mist shrouding the airfield. By the time we got back into the circuit, visibility was down to a few hundred yards. The flare-path lights were clearly visible through the layer of fog, but the ground surface was completely obscured. We touched down, making a rather bumpy landing, as I had held off too high, because of the bad visibility. My crew heaved a great sigh of relief.

There was a complete change of weather the following morning. A front had moved up from the south-west giving extreme cloud cover. This gave the chaps at Group the bright idea that we could do a daylight raid! So, just to keep our hands in, so to speak, it was decided to take advantage of the weather conditions and send us on a 'moling' mission. This was something very different, and we soon discovered, to our concern, what fiendish scheme was being plotted. This was no spectacular mass-formation raid, like that carried out by the American Fortresses. There was no fighter cover, no special training, just the cloud for protection. The weather was expected to be 10/10th cloud up to 10,000 feet all the way to the target area. We hoped that they had got it right this time.

The target was the Ruhr Valley, ostensibly a 'nuisance' raid (22 October 1942). There would be little chance of seeing the target! We were expected to fly on very accurate dead reckoning, and hoped to find a hole in the clouds on ETA. At least we were just as likely to find the target as on some of the night raids. I was happy flying at night, as you felt you had a good chance of not being seen. The night was our friend. I thought the chaps at Group had had a brainstorm. I was sure this was to be a suicide mission. No one was asked to volunteer. It was to be just the same as a night op, but in broad daylight.

Briefing was early and we took off about midday. We were instructed to climb until we were above cloud, and literally skim across the cloud tops. In the event of an attack by fighters, we should immediately descend into the cloud; hence the term 'moling'. We were to rely solely on the protection from the cloud and not to attempt any acts of heroism to engage fighters if we were attacked. However, to give us a feeling of a little more protection, we had beam guns fitted on either side of the fuselage. They were only Vickers .303 and we would have been hopelessly outgunned by fighter cannons. My crew rather relished the idea of the opportunity of shooting down an Me109, but, as luck had it, we did not see a fighter, even in the distance. With the weather below as bad as it was, I doubt if the fighters could have got airborne.

Thus prepared, we set off in thoroughly murky weather; climbing quickly, we broke cloud at about 8,000 feet into brilliant sunshine and clear blue skies above. If we had been standing naked in Piccadilly Circus, we would not have felt more exposed. All eyes were peeled to scan the entire sky for fighters; none appeared. We were rather disappointed, as, although we had been apprehensive about doing this daylight 'stunt', the flight began to get boring, and a little excitement would not have been unwelcome. Still, 'press on regardless chaps!' If the cloud had not broken by the time we reached the target area, we were to return, and in no circumstances were we to drop our bombs without seeing the target. We didn't. After flying for just over two hours, and on ETA, there was no sign of a break in the clouds. I decided to turn back and set course for home. I thought, 'We've not bloody well come all this

way, just to take our bombs back!' So we descended below the cloud
base, broke cloud at about 2,000 feet and looked for a target of opportunity, as it was called – that is, you carry on until you spot something
that looks like a military objective and bomb that. Although we may have
needed something like that for a bit of excitement, I still preferred night
operations, with all its hazards.

After our 'moling' trip over the Ruhr Valley, for the remainder of the
week, the weather was awful. I got off the ground once, when I had to
take a pilot for dual instruction. That day, 27 October, the whole squadron was moved to RAF Kirmington, which had undergone alterations to
provide better facilities.

The weather had improved and we were detailed for another mine-
laying mission (28 October). The target was in the fjord off Stavanger.
Although there was a moon that night, by the time we got halfway across
the North Sea, there was a front lying right across our route, with heavy
cloud down to 1,500 feet, and the night was as black as hell. The low
cloud base did not matter, as we had to come down to about 200 feet to
drop the mine. We stayed below the cloud base all across the North Sea,
but we could not even see the horizon. The night was unbelievably black,
and there was not a break in the clouds. Normally, even on dark nights,
it is possible to pick out the coastline, where the surf is breaking on the
shore, but on this night the sea, sky and land were indistinguishable.

The mountains rose steeply near the coast, and if we could not see the
coastline, there was a real danger of overshooting and flying slap into the
mountains. If we were to drop our mine in the target area, there was
absolutely no room for error. We reached the ETA for the coast, but we
could still see nothing. We had already been in the air for two and a half
hours, and this was the safe limit, unless we could see the coastline. If the
forecast wind had been wrong, and the ground speed underestimated, we
would have overshot the landfall. Moreover, dead reckoning was not all
that accurate, and we were out of range of an RD fix. Realising we must
have been in close proximity to the dropping zone, I decided not to risk
going any further. Relying on my navigator's accuracy, I gave the order
to drop the mine and set course for home. I don't remember ever having
flown on such a totally black night as that.

No. 150 Squadron suffered two losses that night on mine-laying operations.
It was presumed that the Wellington of Australian pilot Flying Officer Crane

was lost over the sea with a total loss of life. The Wellington flown by
Sergeant Woodcock smashed into the Quantock hills; one of the crew was
killed and the other four airmen injured.

We had been briefed to return to Lossiemouth for refuelling and go back
to base immediately that morning. On the flight to base, to relieve the
monotony, we joined up with other aircraft and flew back in formation.

The next ten days were typical November weather and we did not
leave the deck once. I had saved up my ration of petrol, so I took the
opportunity to spend an hour or two in Grimsby, and set off in my baby
Austin, taking my navigator with me. We had a couple of pints at the
Ship, and made back for camp. We arrived at the turn into the Officers'
Mess drive, but in the black-out, and with very little light from the car
headlights, I misjudged the corner. Turning the wheel too sharply, I
caught the front offside wheel on the kerb and promptly turned the car
on its side. As it happened, we were moving quite slowly, and the only
injury I sustained was to my pride. We got out unscathed and surveyed
the sorry sight. There seemed to be little damage done, other than one
broken side window. Together we heaved her up, and to my surprise got
her back on her wheels again. We pressed the starter and, presto, she
started up straight away. We got in and drove back to the Mess, none the
worse for the episode.

The chance of having weather good enough at this time of the year is
pretty slim. We needed good weather for take-off, good weather over the
target, and good weather to land back, even if it meant being diverted.
It was not very often at this time of the year that these three conditions
coincided. The weather conditions over Germany would invariably
determine where the choice of target would be. So it was on 9 November
that the Met chaps saw a fifty–fifty chance of clearance over a target
area, and that there was a chance of a break in the clouds sufficient to
see the target. It was to be Hamburg.

We took off while it was still daylight, in typical November conditions,
with 10/10th cloud cover from about 2,000 feet to 8,000 feet. We climbed
as quickly as possible to get above the murk. Suddenly we broke through
the top of the cloud, into a gloriously breathtaking scene. Today, for
those who fly regularly, it is quite a common experience to see a beautiful
sunset, and it is something that is taken very much for granted. On that
occasion, the sun had just sunk below the horizon, the western sky was a

blaze of colour, and the snow-white tops of the cloud completed the dazzling scene.

Hamburg was notorious for being one of the most heavily defended targets. It was for this reason that I was asked to take a passenger with me. Major Albrecht was an artillery officer, and his intention was to observe German anti-aircraft tactics, and to determine whether there was anything he could learn from them. He little realised that he would be treated to a special performance for his benefit. The cloud persisted over the North Sea, and continued to build up as we neared the German coast. We had hoped to get a good pinpoint from the Frisian Islands, but they were totally obscured by cloud. From that point we soon realised when we had crossed the coast, as the defences opened up, and heavy flak shells started bursting all round us. They were putting up a very heavy barrage, firing blind and relying on direction-finding instruments. This mission was to be a 'maximum effort', and there would be hundreds of aircraft over the target area, the object being to saturate the defences. We were briefed to fly a dog-leg track coming into the south of Hamburg, then turn north to bomb the target, then leave the target area flying west, thus making a one-way traffic over the target area to avoid the risk of collisions.

My passenger took up his position standing in the astrodome, where he could get a good all-round view of what was going on. He was also making detailed notes of the action. I had to admire the cool of the chap. He had not been on a raid before and he was finding out for himself what it was like to be at the other end. The Major was having a field day, as it was certainly one of the heaviest barrages I had experienced so far. There was only broken cloud over the target, so we were able to see scores of bombs going off. Every now and again, there was a much larger explosion when a bomb had hit some particularly vital target. Hundreds of heavy gun flashes were going off all the time. Scores of searchlights were weaving about somewhat aimlessly. The acrid smell of cordite from bursting shells permeated the aircraft. It was easy enough to identify the target, with no light from searchlights reflecting in the water of the harbour. Soon dozens of fires were burning on the ground, creating a scene like Dante's inferno.

Occasionally we would see one of our aircraft caught in searchlights; then all beams would concentrate on this unlucky one, attention being temporarily diverted from the rest of us. From the moment we started the run-up to the target, when the aircraft had to be held straight and level, we were at risk from being picked up by the searchlights. The run-up would not last for more than a few minutes, but it would seem like an eternity. So once the bombs had gone, we did not stick around, getting straight out as quickly as possible. There was probably more risk from collision than from enemy action.

All this time my passenger had been coolly making notes of his observations. He could not have realised how concentrated the flak was. If anyone deserved a gong that night for 'keeping cool in the face of heavy enemy action', he did! The mission took six and a half hours.

Once again we were grounded for the next ten days, as the weather made flying impossible. We did not even carry out a normal air test before preparing for our next mission.

After Hamburg it was quite a relief to be on mine-laying again off Saint-Nazaire (19 November). These sorties were relatively easy, as for most of the route there would be no flak. There was a full moon this night, and flying across Brittany at about 10,000 feet we were not troubled with any enemy opposition. Visibility was good, and we had no difficulty in finding the mouth of the river Loire. There was, however, quite a lot of light flak as we flew up the estuary to the dropping zone, but at low level we had no difficulty in avoiding it.

As we had flown direct from base, the round trip had lasted five hours. So, rather than attempt to make it back to base, we were diverted to St Eval in Cornwall for refuelling. St Eval was probably the most desolate airfield in the country. Almost on the tip of Land's End, it was a grim god forsaken spot blasted by the full force of Atlantic gales. It was another two hours' flight back to base, so there would have been no possibility of making the full return flight without refuelling. We were soon refuelled and ready to return. We had no wish to stay there a moment longer than necessary. It was not until we took off in daylight that we saw that at the end of the runway there was a sheer drop of 200–300 feet. If you overshot, you went over the edge of the cliff into the sea.

On the night of 22–3 November 1942 RAF Bomber Command sent a force of 222 aircraft to attack Stuttgart. No. 150 Squadron detailed eleven aircraft to join in the attack, 'but two were cancelled prior to take-off', as reported in the Squadron ORB. The exact reason is not recorded, but one of the respective crews had been scrubbed by Richard Pinkham.

A few days later we were briefed to hit Stuttgart. This was to be the deepest penetration we had attempted on Wellington IIIs. There did not appear to be anything remarkable about this mission, other than that it would be a long flight; otherwise, it was not very different from all the other sorties. Briefing was early, and we were to operate from an advance base at Oakington. While the aircraft were being refuelled we had a good meal, with a couple of hours' relaxation before going out to our aircraft, which were all lined up wing-tip to wing-tip around the perimeter track to the east of the airfield.

Oakington was a Stirling wing, but this night the squadron were stood down, and their ground crews looked after refuelling our aircraft and ensuring that everything was ready for take-off. As senior officer in charge of the squadron that night, half an hour before take-off I checked all our crews to satisfy myself that everything was in order. I went along the line of aircraft, to make a last-minute check and give the OK to get on board and start up engines. No problems, so I made my way back to my own kite. Halfway back I came across a huddle of ground crews just in front of one of our aircraft. Their attention was concentrated on the ground, where I saw what they were looking at. Some poor airman had walked into one of the turning props, one side of his head being completely cut off. The 'blood wagon' appeared promptly on the scene and a medical orderly got out and examined the dead airman. Part of the dead man's brains had spilled out on to the tarmac, and casually the orderly picked them up and tossed them back into his skull.

The pilot of this aircraft had just started up one of his engines, and the ground crew were moving round to the other side, when one of them had walked into the spinning propeller. The Oakington ground crews were used to walking around under the Stirlings, with the prop tips a good two feet clear above their heads. Sadly this poor sod had forgotten that Wimpeys were very much lower, and of course in the dark he would not have seen the spinning prop.

The pilot of that plane was badly shaken, and I told him to scrub his mission. He would have been in no fit state to carry out his operational duties. Fortunately none of the other pilots was aware of the accident, and I made my way back to my own kite. I was just about to get in, when an operations officer came along and handed me a slip of rice paper. (All secret orders were written on rice paper, which the recipient had to swallow as soon as he had read the instructions.)

Met had come up with a last-minute forecast warning of vapour trails at normal operational heights, and with the brilliant moon and clear sky we would have been sitting ducks for night-fighters. The instructions were quite explicit: 'Cross the French coast at 12,000 feet. Descend immediately to 300 feet above ground level. Fly all the way to the target at that height. Climb to bombing height on approaching the target area. After dropping the bombs descend to 300 feet above ground level. Climb to 12,000 feet to cross the French Coast.' In addition we were given a last-minute change of route. We had to make a dog-leg track via Rheims, turn on a course of 080 degrees and set course for Stuttgart. The route was planned to avoid the most inhabited area in France and to avoid high ground. The reason for the unusual variations to the normal briefing was to keep as clear as possible from fighters and heavily defended towns.

We had never had any special training in low-level flying at night, so we had to keep a sharp look-out for any possible obstructions and high ground. However, with the brilliant moonlight we could see the ground almost like daylight. It was really quite exhilarating. Every now and again the ground would rise up, and we climbed to keep a safe height. Once electricity pylons loomed up and I had to pull back smartly to get over them. The rest of the flight went according to plan. We climbed to bomb the target, which in the moonlight stood out like a sore thumb. There was a certain amount of flak over the target area, but they were probably not expecting us, as we had flown this dog-leg track, which feinted as though we were heading for another target, probably Milan.

On the return flight we descended again to keep to 300 feet above the ground. We flew over a concentration of light flak, but at 300 feet at night there was not much chance of them getting a good aim at us, and we were soon out of the danger area. Crossing the French coast, we encountered some light opposition. With all this climbing and low-level flying, our fuel consumption had been considerably increased, and I was getting anxious about our safe limit. After crossing the French coast, we set course for Oakington, where we landed with barely fifteen minutes' supply left. The whole trip had taken six hours fifty minutes.

At the end of the week, I was given fourteen days' leave. I had been home for only four days when I received a telegram: 'Return to unit immediately.' On 2 December 1942 I reported to my unit, to be confronted with the news that the squadron was to be sent to North Africa to help with the Allied landing in Algeria. The squadron was given forty-eight hours in which to prepare for the move.

The raid to Stuttgart on 22 November 1942 brought to an end Richard's operational flying in the United Kingdom. Richard's logbook recorded 44 operations against enemy targets, raids on which 240 bombers had failed to return. Each of these aircraft had been crewed by either five or six men, most of whom had lost their lives. Richard's statistical chances of survival had been one in five, and he maintains that he was lucky and that he had been favoured by fortune. But skill and ability had played their part in skewing the odds in his favour. For the rest of the war the bomber offensive against Germany would escalate to unprecedented levels of destruction, and Bomber Command's casualty figures grew steadily, until by the end of the war the Air Ministry had informed the next of kin of 55,500 airmen that their sons or husbands would not be returning.

But Richard Pinkham would no longer be taking part in the battles of attrition over Germany. His operational future and flying career lay elsewhere, providing new challenges and new opportunities.

The whole squadron was re-equipped with brand new Wellington IIIs, with Hercules XI engines, specially modified with air filters for use in dusty conditions. All crews were kitted out with khaki drill uniform, bed rolls and camp kit. Everyone had to be given appropriate injections.

Then the station MO dropped a bombshell on me, pointing out that I was still medical category A2hBh, 'Operational flying, home service only'. I was not at all happy about the prospect of being separated from my squadron. I asked the MO if he could arrange a medical examination for me, to have me recategorised as 'fit for overseas duties'. He thought that at such short notice it would not be possible to arrange it. I got on the blower to Group and spoke to the Group Medical Officer, to see if he could use his influence to arrange a medical for me. By midday the following day I received word that I should report to the Central Medical Board at Kelvin House, Cleveland Street, Tottenham Court Road.

I caught the 1320 train from Barnetby that afternoon. The following morning I reported to the CMB at 0800 hours. I was sent immediately for an interview with the Chief Medical Officer, who was expecting me. Obviously my MO friend at Group HQ had done his stuff. The interview lasted no more than ten minutes.

'Well how are you feeling now?'

'Absolutely fine, thanks,' I replied.

'No further problems with the headaches?'

'None at all.'

'You look pretty fit to me, but I suppose I had better check your blood pressure and pulse. Roll up your sleeve. Good. Blood pressure OK. Pulse OK. Now step up and down on that chair twenty times! . . . fine you'll live. A2B.'

'Thank you.' I nearly felt like hugging him.

I was back at camp by the afternoon, and lost no time in collecting my kit. Everyone else had been issued with theirs. In addition we were also issued with revolvers, and Army-type boots. There were also emergency rations, cooking utensils, cutlery, plates and water bottles. I began to think we were being prepared for a mission to cross the Sahara.

In the meantime, while I had been away, there had been feverish activity on camp. New aircraft had been flown in, in quick succession – beautiful brand-new kites straight from the manufacturer. They were immediately given a thorough maintenance check: compasses were swung; guns and ammo installed. When this had all been done, the aircraft had to be air-tested. However, despite all the hurry to get ready, the weather was against us.

On the Saturday we were still hard at it, with last-minute checks and briefing, drawing maps and preparing flight plans. But, by Sunday morning, the 6th, we were on stand-by, just waiting for Met clearance. The 7th passed and there was no let up in the weather. Tuesday, the 8th, and there was still no improvement. We did, however, manage to get off the ground and carry out an air test for thirty minutes. With brand new aircraft, thirty minutes were not really sufficient to make sure that everything was handling perfectly. Wednesday, the 9th, we got the order to take off. We would land at Portreath in Cornwall for refuelling, then land at Gibraltar for further refuelling. Destination Blida, Algeria.

I had recollections of a previous visit to Portreath, but this time it was different; it was December. Winds of 30 to 35 knots and gusting to 40 knots south-westerly were the norm. It would have been almost the limit of our range to reach Gibraltar with a favourable wind; we had no choice but to wait for the wind to change. So we waited, and waited. Thursday conditions deteriorated even further, and was not fit for flying at all. Friday it was still not fit. Saturday we were put on stand-by and did another air test, and still we did not get the OK to go. Instead of the weather improving, it got decidedly worse. We were thoroughly brassed off. We were living in huts that were very draughty and leaking, with only a Tortoise stove to heat the large hut, with almost forty blokes trying to get near the stove to get warm. The stove got red hot and those near it were scorched, while those who could not get near were frozen. Day after day was cold and wet, with Atlantic gales blowing. They were the most miserable nine days.

On Friday, the 18th, the wind veered to the north-west, so, before it had a chance to change again, we got ready to get airborne at midnight. We taxied out to take-off position, and checked the engine magneto switches. The port engine was OK, but the mag on the starboard engine showed a drop of 300–400 revs. Normally this would have been a good enough reason to scrub the take-off, but the prospect of spending another night at Portreath did not appeal to me. I thought that, as long as one mag was OK, we should be all right, and probably the other mag would clear itself after we had been in the air for some time. It was in fact a reckless risk. If one engine had failed, we could have been in serious trouble. With a maximum load, at night, it does not bear thinking about the consequences.

We got airborne all right, and raised the undercarriage and flaps, but when I attempted to adjust the elevator trim I found it had stuck. I had carried out a full pre-flight check and everything had been functioning normally. For some time I was struggling to hold the nose down, but eventually it dawned on me what was the cause of the trouble. Something must have jammed the trim control cables. The last man to board the aircraft had pulled up the ladder and stowed it in the wrong position. Somehow it had fouled the trim control cables. The ladder was released and we all heaved a sigh of relief, as I adjusted the trim control and set course for Gib.

To avoid upsetting the Portuguese, we prepared a flight plan to fly out over the Bay of Biscay, parallel to the coast of Portugal, and then to fly on a course due east for Gib. The wind turned out to be much stronger than forecast, and by the time we were supposed to be west of Cape Finisterre it was starting to get daylight, and to my horror I found we were over land. I soon realised that we were in fact over Portugal! There seemed little point in flying back out to sea again, as everyone below would probably be asleep, and I thought they would hardly send a fighter up to intercept us. Besides we did not have enough fuel to make a detour. There was not a cloud in the sky, so we settled down to enjoy the unfamiliar vista of the red earth of Portugal.

The sight of the 'Rock' was most reassuring, and we put down at Gibraltar after flying for five hours and fifty minutes, which did not leave us with too much fuel to spare. While the aircraft were being refuelled, we tucked into a very good breakfast. As soon as my fitter had eaten, he hurried to check the magnetos, and found one of the contact rockers had stuck. The fault was soon rectified and we were ready for the next leg. There was no time for sightseeing at Gibraltar. Once again we were on our way, with another two hours' flight, destination Blida. The coast of Africa soon loomed up, but our first impression was of a very menacing-looking mountain range, rising to about 5,000 feet: the Atlas mountains. To my astonishment the airfield was separated from the foothills of the mountains only by the sprawling town of Blida! I had nasty visions of returning from a sortie in bad weather, with a mountain too close for comfort.

7. North Africa

The German land armies in North Africa were being squeezed into a corner. At El Alamein in late October 1942 the British Eighth Army launched the offensive that initiated the Allied drive west, and early in November Allied forces landed on the shores of north-west Africa and began their push east. Through the early months of 1943 enemy armour and troops fell back, eventually making their last stand on Tunisian soil. The overwhelming Allied fighting power meant it was only a matter of time before the German and Italian presence in North Africa was extinguished. Hitler, however, did not have the foresight to appreciate the futility of continuing the Tunisian battle, and the supply lines to the Axis troops were kept open. When Richard Pinkham arrived in North Africa at the end of 1942, he, along with his squadron colleagues, would be tasked with battering and breaking those supply lines.

No. 150 Squadron, RAF Blida, North Africa

It soon became apparent that conditions were now going to be very different from what we had been accustomed to. The airfield was a dusty barren patch of ground, with no runway, perimeter track or hard standings. There was not a speck of green vegetation to be seen anywhere. Landing and take-off could be made only in either an easterly or a westerly direction, parallel to the range of the mountains. The prevailing wind was westerly, so whenever it was in that direction we would have to do a right-hand circuit.

We joined the circuit, and immediately got a 'green' from the airfield controller. We made our approach and landing, picking out a clear space, and avoiding getting too close to any of the numerous aircraft parked all round the perimeter. Again I wondered, 'What would happen if we had starboard engine failure. There could be no hope of doing a right-hand circuit, and to attempt to do a left-hand circuit would take us much too close to the mountains and right over the town.' It could have been very dodgy, to say the least.

We were allocated accommodation in the French Air Force barracks. I was lucky; I had to share a room only with two other officers. We settled in as quickly as possible. The billets were very spartan. Sanitation was primitive. And December in North Africa could be very cold at night. We had to scavenge for firewood, to provide any warmth. Even the Nissen huts back in England were comparative luxury. We had all been issued with camp kit in England, which comprised a folding canvas camp-bed, canvas hand wash bowl and canvas bath. There was also a canvas folding chair. The only thing you could say was that at least we were in brick buildings, and that conditions in the desert would have been ten times worse.

John Kirwan was made the squadron commander, and promoted to Wing Commander. He was a very likeable chap, and was very popular with all ranks. Squadron Leader Holmes was 'A' flight commander, and I was 'B' flight commander. We had a really first-class bunch of chaps, both aircrew and ground crew. There was a terrific team spirit in the squadron.

For three days before Christmas we carried out air tests. There was no time to lose, but the war stopped for Christmas. Then on the 28th we did another air test, and this time the aircraft were bombed-up ready for our first attack on Bizerta in Tunisia. This turned out to be a piece of cake! The target was the docks. The flak was no problem. The target was easy to identify. We were over enemy territory for at most half an hour. We were back at base within five hours.

The weather held good for the whole of January, so I was able to get in seven ops during the month. The target was always Bizerta, and became known as the 'milk run'. We gave Bizerta docks a hell of a pounding, as this was the main supply source for the German Army.

Most of the time weather forecasting was very reliable, as conditions in January were usually very good. If we were not detailed for ops for any particular night, we would take the evening off and spend the time in one of the cafés in Blida town. My greatest concern was to find somewhere to get a bath. There were no facilities for bathing at the camp. The canvas bowls we had were about 2-feet square. So a proper bath became a priority search. Eventually we managed to persuade the manager of the Hotel Orient to let us have regular baths at the hotel.

On 14 January the CO decided to 'have a bash', so I was stood down and he took my aircraft and crew. I tried to persuade him not to take my kite, as I believed it was unlucky for anyone else to fly my aircraft. Sure enough the weather clamped down. They got into difficulties and had to bale out. The Wingco landed on the side of a mountain and broke his leg. The others got down safely. Consequently, as a result of his injury, he had to go to hospital, and, as I was senior flight commander, I became acting squadron commander.

It was about this time that the station commander sent for me and told me the squadron had been allocated a dozen gongs. Would I nominate whom I could recommend for decorations, and write out suitable citations. I found it difficult to select twelve chaps who were more deserving than the rest. They all merited distinction. I selected the names of those who had served the longest with the squadron and presented my list of names to the station commander.

'Where's your name Squadron Leader?' he enquired. 'It's about time you got a gong!' 'Modesty forbids,' I thought. But before I could answer he said, 'Add your name to the list, and write your own citation!' Fortunately the secret was between him and me. I dread to think how I would have been ragged if the chaps had known I had written my own citation.

Eventually Wing Commander Malan was posted to take command of the squadron. Although I had been acting CO, I could not have expected to be made CO; for one thing I did not have sufficient seniority and moreover I was nearing the end of my tour.

On 18 January 1943 we went to Bizerta and then again on 20 January. By this time we had done the milk run to Bizerta so often, we had become almost contemptuous of the defences over the target. Regularly we went in at 7,000 feet, which was about the limit of their light flak. On 20 January there was a full moon and we got a perfect night photograph of our bombs actually dropping towards the target. We were credited with a direct hit on dock installations, which was confirmed by photographic reconnaissance next day.

Thursday evening, 21 January, there was no flying, as, although there was a cloudless sky, gale-force winds were forecast. Instead we were entertained by an American concert party with 'Four Jills and a Jeep'. They were Kay Francis, Carol Landis, Martha Raye and Mitzi Mayfair. After the show they were entertained in the Sergeants' Mess, which we felt was 'rank' discrimination.

We enjoyed the services of the first-class catering staff, and the imagination with which they served up corned beef at every meal was quite remarkable. We lived on corned beef every day, for breakfast, lunch and supper, but I can honestly say I never got tired of corned beef.

On 23 January 1943 it was Bizerta again. We had been warned that there were large movements of enemy armour in Tunisia. We had dropped our bombs, and when we were well clear of the target area I brought her down to about 500 feet to look for any possible signs of enemy activity. We could see the ground as clear as daylight in the brilliant moonlight. Sure enough we found a column of transport, so the chaps in the front and rear turrets fired off all their ammo at the vehicles. They were sitting ducks, and we must have made a real mess of their transport.

On the 26th, Flight Lieutenant Summers, our intelligence officer, and I went into Blida and had a meal at the Regal restaurant. It was a nice change to get away from our staple diet of corned beef. However, food was in desperately short supply, as the Germans had pretty well cleared the country of food. The only choices on the menu were liver and omelettes. The French cuisine lived up to its reputation well, and it was an education to see what they could do with eggs and liver. The dessert was invariably oranges, of which there was unlimited supply. We never suffered with constipation. Frequently we would have a fry-up in the billet. Young local boys, who always hung around the camp, would be sent off to bring back a couple of dozen oranges and as many eggs – a perfectly balanced diet, you could say.

Following another raid on Bizerta in the night of 29–30 January 1943, we attacked Trapani, Sicily, on 31 January–1 February. Concentrations of supplies were being prepared at Trapani for the German forces in Tunisia. We were required to destroy these supplies, vital to Rommel's army, which was gradually being squeezed into a corner as the Eighth and First Armies closed in from east and west. It was not an easy task to find storage dumps at night. The target was well illuminated by parachute flares, but it was very difficult to get a good pinpoint. The target was just about at the limit of our range, so we did not have any spare time to stooge around looking for it. The round trip took over six hours. Had we got short of fuel we could have landed at fighter airfields near the front, but they did not have facilities for handling our Wimpeys, so we made every effort to return to base.

At the start of February the weather was beginning to deteriorate, which considerably curtailed our activities, but we were briefed to stand by for a very vital op. A large convoy of desperately needed supplies had to get through to the Eighth Army, but were threatened by attack from Junker 88s based on Sardinia. We had to attack the Junkers' airbase at Villacidro.

The one occasion when we could have really put on a good show, the weather was against us. For twenty-four hours a strong Sirocco wind from the south made take-off impossible. Taking off to the south was much too dangerous. It would have involved making a steep turn to port immediately after take-off, to avoid flying into the mountains. Despite the well-known risk, all our chaps were eager to have a bash, but the station commander considered it was much too dangerous. If an aircraft stalled in a steep turn after take-off, it would have crashed into Blida town.

On 7 February the wind changed and we got clearance to take off. The target was the aerodrome at Villacidro, and our task was to keep the German bombers grounded, to prevent them attacking the convoy. As our new CO had not had any experience on Wimpeys, I took him with me on this trip. There was a lot of cloud about, and the aerodrome was well inland, with no easily identifiable landmarks. Our chaps were milling around dropping flares all over the place. We found a few clearances in the cloud, but we could not risk coming below the cloud base, as there were mountains up to 4,000 feet in the vicinity. We spent a lot of time trying to find gaps in the cloud. Even if we could not find the aerodrome to bomb it, at least as long as we stooged around, the German Air Force did not dare to illuminate its flare path, for its aircraft to take off. We continued to stooge around for nearly an hour, forcing Jerry to keep his head down. We received a gratifying report that the Jerry bombers had not attacked the convoy.

We carried out another successful attack on Bizerta on 13 February. It was a late take-off, and by the time we had left the target, the sky was already beginning to get light as we set course for base. It had not been a very exciting raid – just quickly in and then a quick getaway. As we were still over enemy-occupied territory when it became daylight, the possibility of fighter interception occurred to me, although there had been no reports of fighters then. Nevertheless I did not see any point in hanging around to find out. I did wonder how we might have coped if we had been attacked. I decided to get out of the danger area as quickly as possible. This was a good opportunity to find out just what speed I could get out of the Wimpey. Putting the nose down in a shallow descent, I opened up the throttles to full boost. We reached a speed on the clock of 245 knots, which I maintained for half an hour. The whole kite was shuddering like a jelly, and the wings with their flexible construction were vibrating vigorously. I held her straight and level at that speed for half an hour. On return to base I taxied over to dispersal and asked 'Chiefy' to give the engines a thorough check over, particularly the oil filters. He was not pleased that I had treated his aircraft so roughly. However, he assured me that there were no visible signs of stress on the engines, which more than upheld the reputation of these very remarkable Hercules engines.

After that the weather really clamped down, and the forecast was that it would remain as bad for the next week at least. This was the signal for a squadron all-ranks party. Everyone got thoroughly pissed. That night there was a very heavy fall of snow on the mountain. As we had not had a break since we arrived in Algeria, I put in for a few days' leave. I told the CO I would like to go to Chréa, a ski resort at the top of the mountain, to get in some skiing if conditions were suitable. He said he would have no objection, provided I kept in touch with him by phone each day, and that, if there was anything on, I should return immediately. I took a Jeep and, as no one else wanted to ski, I went up on my own. Conditions were quite good, and I hired a pair of skis, kitted myself out and set off. It was good to get away, and I quite enjoyed being on my own, to commune with God and nature. The utter stillness and silence were quite elevating. There was no wind and not the slightest sound from the trees, nor the sound of a bird; because the snow was fresh, there was not even the swish from my skis.

I skied along on the level through the woods, just going wherever I fancied. I had been going along like this for about an hour, when I could just detect the faintest sound of music. I thought I must be hallucinating. Who on earth could be out here in the wilderness, miles from any sign of habitation. There were no chalets anywhere in sight. I continued in the general direction from where the sound appeared to be coming. As I did so, the sound became louder. I recognised the music of Debussy. It was quite enthralling. I still could not believe my ears. Suddenly through the trees I spotted a wooden chalet. This was the source of this heavenly music. As I got nearer, it was unmistakably the sound of a piano, being played by a maestro of exceptional talent. I peered through a window, and there, quite oblivious of my presence, was a beautiful young woman.

She was startled and stopped playing as I knocked on the window. She turned her head towards me, and in not very good French I suggested: 'Je voudrais bien vous entendre jouer.' It was good enough, for the reply was 'Entrez'. I told her I was absolutely enthralled to hear the sound of such beautiful music and in such a remote and isolated place. Would she mind if I stayed and listened for a while? 'D'accord,' she graciously replied.

She explained that she was practising for a concert to be held in Algiers, in aid of French refugees in Algeria. She had come up to this quiet spot, where she could practise undisturbed. The chalet was sparsely furnished, and a small oil stove was the sole source of heat. I stayed and listened to her for an hour or so until it was starting to get dark, and I decided it was time to take my leave. I thanked her and said goodbye. I am sure no one at the concert enjoyed her performance more than I did.

I spent four days skiing; on the fifth day, when I phoned the CO, he said, 'You are wanted!' That was all I needed to know, and within half an hour I was back at base. The weather had not completely cleared up, but I was able to carry out an air test, and on the 22nd we were off again on the milk run. I got another good photograph of the docks at Bizerta, and scored a direct hit.

The following day, DFCs and DFMs were awarded to the squadron, which was the signal for a really big celebration. As if we had not had enough drink that night, the following night we were invited to a party given by the French officers and their wives.

The next night I was duty officer in charge of night flying, so the rest of the squadron went off without me. The weather was very bad, and we lost another kite, because of the weather that night.

The French Air Force had two squadrons of old Farman bi-plane bombers, based at Blida airfield. They were obsolete and quite unfit for operational flying. It was really tragic, because the Wimpeys looked so much more modern and businesslike. It was quite humiliating for the French Air Force personnel.

At the party with the French officers the previous night, I had met one of the officers, Lieutenant Marcel de Gironde, who had expressed interest in our aircraft, and I offered to take him on a flight the next morning. I had to do an air test in the morning, so it was a good opportunity for him to come up with us. Being cut off from their supplies for spares, they had resorted to carrying out improvised maintenance, literally 'wire and string'. We were really very sorry for them, because they were so envious of our magnificent aircraft.

Lieutenant de Gironde was quite thrilled and very impressed by his trip with us. Apart from this isolated episode, we had nothing at all to do with the French personnel on an official basis, just the occasional social drink at their private quarters.

For a change from the milk run (we had bombed Bizerta again on 23 February) we were briefed to have a bash at Tunis on 2 March. There could not have been much of Bizerta left, as we had pounded it cease-lessly for two months. So Tunis was a nice change. It was an uneventful trip; the opposition was ineffectual. It was again already getting light as we left the target area, and by the time we had passed out of Tunisia I handed over the controls to my navigator, as I had decided I needed to go back and have a 'leak'. As I returned to the cockpit I stuck my head up in the astrodome to look at the beautiful dawn breaking.

As I looked forward, I saw what looked like a chimney sticking out of the fuselage! For a moment I could not figure it out. Nobody had told me of any modification that had been carried out on the aircraft. I had not a clue. I went forward to examine it more closely and I could not believe my eyes. All the chaps on our squadron went in to bomb at 7,000 feet, whereas our 'sister' squadron preferred to go in at least 10,000 feet. The chance in a million had happened. One of the parachute flares had been released by one of their kites and the casing had fallen on our kite, and stuck in the fuselage – only a few inches behind where my head would have been. It was bad enough having the enemy throwing things at us, but to have something dropped on us from one of our own aircraft was not amusing.

For the whole of the next week, ops were scrubbed because of bad weather.

On 7 March there was a big ceremony of presentation of the colours to the French contingent. I had the honour of representing the Royal Air Force at saluting base. My smattering of French probably gave me the opportunity.

To give us something to do, we did a bit of 'fighter liaison'. There was a fighter staging wing with Hurricanes nearby at Maison Blanche, where pilots were held in reserve awaiting posting to squadrons. We were asked to give these chaps the opportunity to get in some simulation attacks. The general idea was for us to do some evasive action, while the Hurricanes would carry out mock attacks. It was great fun until we got tired of pissing around, when we decided to turn the tables on them. We could outclimb the Hurricanes and turn inside their turn, so we usually ended up 'attacking' them.

There followed several days of very heavy rain and the surface of the airfield became a quagmire. It was just impossible to operate in those conditions. Fortunately, as soon as the sun came out again the ground quickly dried as hard as rock.

We were detailed to stand by for another attack on Tunis (12 March 1943). When you look at the map of North Africa, the distance from Algiers to Tunis does not seem to be very far, but the last trip there had taken six hours. This time, however, it took only five hours and thirty-five minutes. We were lucky we did not have to stooge around before finding the target. Getting to the target area was relatively simple. Finding the exact target and making a steady run-up to the precise dropping spot were not so simple. We often had to make the run-up to the target two, three and sometimes even four times to be absolutely sure of getting it. This time we went in and out in no time at all.

By now I was getting impatient to finish my tour. This trip to Tunis would be my fifty-ninth op. Only one more to go. Two of my most experienced pilots had already completed the statutory thirty ops on this tour, but both implored me to allow them to continue, so that they could remain with their crews, who had done less than the required tour number. They wanted to stay on until their crew had completed their tours. They went off one night and one of them did not return. I decided that the other should be taken off ops immediately, as I did not want to lose him also. He was quite angry with me for taking him off, but I prevailed.

The 16th was a red-letter day for me. My Distinguished Flying Cross was promulgated and, of course, there was great celebrating, with everyone wanting to buy me a drink. Next morning I had the king of all hangovers! This was followed by two more days of absolutely foul weather. But in a way I was not sorry that we were grounded, after my prize hangover.

Supplement to *London Gazette*, Tuesday, 13 April 1943.

The King has been graciously pleased to approve the following awards in recognition of gallantry displayed in flying operations against the enemy: *Distinguished Flying Cross*

Acting Squadron Leader Richard Mansfield Pinkham (42765). No. 150
Squadron.

This officer has completed 56 sorties during which he has attacked
targets in Germany, Italy and Tunisia. He has at all times pressed home his
mission with the utmost courage and determination and has obtained many
excellent photographs. Squadron Leader Pinkham has invariably displayed
exceptional skill and keenness and has contributed materially to the many
successes achieved by his squadron.

On 20 March 1943, the weather having lifted with only scattered clouds,
the target was Ferryville, a few miles west of Bizerta, but well out of the
defences of Bizerta. It was a round trip of just over five hours. Then on
21 March the target was the airfield at El Moua Sfax. This is located on
the east coast of Tunisia well to the south. The route took us inland and
over the mountains. So, to keep well clear of the mountains, we went out
at 10,000 feet but came down to 7,000 feet to get a good sight of the
aerodrome. I recalled our ordeal at Driffield and hoped our bombing
was as accurate as Jerry's attack on Driffield. We returned without
incident. Then on 1 April 1943 it was Bizerta again! Surely there could
not be anything left to bomb. In fact, there was a lot of cloud cover over
the target, and we could not be certain that we had hit the target. I had
hoped to do one more op to complete my tour, but the CO decided that
I had done enough and this proved to be my last op.

On the night of the 12th one of our aircraft had had to make a forced
landing in some remote spot, just inside the border of Tunisia. They
were all safe, but the kite had to be abandoned as they could not take off
on the rough territory. The crew had been rescued by an Army
detachment and taken to a fighter airfield. I was all set to go and pick up
the crew, but was not permitted to do so, as it was considered too near
enemy lines, and a Wimpey was not considered capable of defending
itself against fighters. So I had the ignominy of being taken to the airfield
at Souk el Khemis in a USAAF B-17 Flying Fortress!

We flew in one of our aircraft to Telergma, which was a US Air Force
base, from where I was to be taken by the B-17. A Captain Teague was
more than pleased to demonstrate the superiority of their aircraft to the
'Goddam Limeys'. Their whole attitude was one of complete
nonchalance. They made absolutely no flight plan, and we just headed
in an easterly direction. I sat up front with the pilot. There were clearly

no defined landmarks, but their method of navigation was simple. As we passed over valleys and ridges the navigator would say, 'No, I don't think this is the one. Keep going Mac.' We passed over another ridge, but he said, 'No, it does not look like this one!' I pointed out that we were now over Tunisia. 'OK, Buddy!' I had my own map, but map reading was extremely difficult with few prominent landmarks. In fact we were well off track, but I could see a ridge of mountains to our port, which I was fairly certain I could identify as the Monte de la Medjerda, with the valley to the south. We made an alteration of course of about 30 degrees to starboard, and from there we followed the river, which took us to Souk el Khemis. We landed, picked up our chaps and headed back to Telergma. I thought, 'Thank God, I had a good navigator!' His navigator seemed to be completely clueless.

Feelings against the Yanks had been running high among the British forces. They arrived in North Africa with the attitude that they would show us how to win this 'Goddam war'. They thought they knew it all, and our own men resented it. Feelings reached a high point, and became so bad that a Command Order was issued to the effect that any of our forces uttering any derogatory remarks against the Yanks would be put on a charge and face possible courts martial.

I got back to Blida with our rescued crew, none the worse for the experience of flying with the Yanks. On returning to our flight I was informed that my tour was finished and that I was posted back home. I was told to arrange my own passage and that if I could get on an aircraft going to England I could go with them if they had room for me. I was anxious to get back as soon as possible, as my wife was expecting our second child almost any day, and naturally I wanted to be with her for the birth.

I spent a week hanging around Maison Blanche trying to 'thumb' a lift, but without any luck. So I decided to take matters into my own hands. No one appeared to know where I was or where I should be going. Moreover, no one seemed to care. I might have to stick around Algiers indefinitely. Even the embarkation officer had no record of my posting. After some 'belly-aching' to this officer, I was told that the *Duchess of York* would be sailing on 23 April and that I could get a berth on that ship.

Six days out over the Bay of Biscay we were attacked by a Focke-Wulf 200 'Condor'. I had been appointed deck officer and was keeping watch. In the event of emergency I was responsible for mustering passengers for boarding the lifeboats at our station. I watched the Condor making his bombing run, fascinated by the thought that for a change I was on the receiving end. It made two bombing runs at about 10,000 feet missing both times. I was even mentally saying 'Left, left, steady.' I thought to myself, 'He's off target!' Suddenly there was a tremendous fountain of water off our starboard, about 100 yards away. After this little excitement, the rest of the trip was uneventful, and we docked at Liverpool on 2 May.

I got through disembarkation like lightning. I had brought back with me a Kashmir Lynx fur coat, a beautiful blue and white sapphire gold bracelet, linen, silks and wool for Marie. I held my breath through customs fully expecting to pay duty on all the 'luxury' goods, but they were not in the slightest bit interested. I heaved a great sigh of relief as I cleared customs, and headed for Southport, where I arrived at the nursing home at four in the afternoon to find that Marie had given birth to a boy, whom we called John, on 26 April.

I hung around for a month, waiting for a posting. At least I was able to make up for lost time with my family, and enjoy a spell of leave at Southport. Eventually I got a telegram to report to No. 82 Operational Training Unit RAF Ossington.

8. Preparing the Airmen

When reading through Richard's account of his time at No. 82 Operational Training Unit, the perils of training should always be kept in mind. Over 8,000 Bomber Command personnel lost their lives on non-operational duties, the majority of these in training accidents. It was a staggering number of fatalities.

Excerpts from the No. 82 OTU ORB provide the matter-of-fact details of some of the training casualties while Richard was with the unit.

21 August: 2327 hrs. Wellington HE 332. J., Capt. F/Sgt Shaw, H.C. crashed on approach to land on edge of Airfield. P/O F. G. Ingham (Navigator) and Sgt. R. W. Hughes (A/B) were killed. Remaining 4 members of crew received minor injuries. Aircraft Cat. E. Aircraft hit top of tree on approach.

24 August: 1100 hrs. Wellington III BK 399. W. Burnt out at dispersal. Aircraft preparing to taxy out for a flight. One of crew fired Verey pistol which he did not know was loaded. Inquiry being held by S/Ldr Haworth-Booth. No injuries to crew. Two crash tenders and domestic fire tender were at the scene of the fire within a few minutes but the fire had already got too great a hold to save the aircraft. Newark N.F.S. also attended.

22 November 1943: 1 aircraft detailed for a Nickel operation according to 93 Group Operation Order No. B8. Target St. Malo. This aircraft 'B' LN 601 Wellington X crashed on take-off. All crew killed. Aircraft burned out. Captain Sgt. Johnson. F/Lt Brassington, gunnery leader, was flying as mid-upper gunner.

W. R. Chorley, in his book *Royal Air Force Bomber Command Losses*

Volume 7: Operational Training Units 1940–1947,[1] recorded further:

> T/o 2158 Desborough with the intention to drop leaflets in the
> St. Nazaire region of France but having climbed to a mere 800 feet,
> the port engine failed and the [Wellington] plunged to the ground at
> Norwell Woods House near Kneeshall Lodge. On impact, there was an
> explosion as the bomber went up in flames.

> 11 December 1943: 2305 hours. Wellington X HE.460 'A' crashed and
> burned out, 10 miles North-west of Little Rissington, Gloucester. Captain
> Sgt. Di Domenico and remainder of crew injured. Sgt Young killed.
> Starboard engine cut at 9,000 feet when Air Bomber at controls.
> Captain took over aircraft, lost 4,000 feet in this operation, and pilot
> could not gain control. Ordered bale out at 2,800 feet but crew
> considered too low. Aircraft hit tree – crashed and fired.

No. 82 OTU, RAF Ossington

RAF Ossington had not long been in operation as an Operational Training Unit when I arrived on 5 June 1943. I was posted as flight commander instructing Canadian aircrews on Wellingtons.

They had all done their advance flying training in Canada, but had not been subject to the standard of discipline that the Royal Air Force had been accustomed to expect. In fact, they turned out to be a 'right shower'. Not only did they lack any discipline; they were also totally lacking in any of the enthusiasm that we had.

After a couple of months two more flights were formed, and my flight and another were transferred to the satellite airfield at Gamston, just south of Retford. Much of my time was spent setting training schedules, and trying to instil into these boys from the backwoods of Canada the rudiments of discipline. We had to get them through a very tight training programme and make sure that when they left us they would be fully competent to fly on operations. It meant cracking the whip to get aircraft in the air at every opportunity.

My staff and I had to be constantly kicking their backsides to get them into the air on time, to get them to turn up punctually for lectures, ground training and the 'Link'. They were a lazy bunch. I would find them sitting round the fire in the Officers' Mess lounge with the fire dying out, and not one of them would get up to put more coal on the fire! Most of them were rather apathetic and indifferent. They had volunteered for the Air Force rather than be conscripted into the Army. They were attracted to the glamour and better pay.

Although my staff instructors ensured that the trainees received full and proper training, the Canadians lacked the zeal to which we had been accustomed in the Royal Air Force aircrew.

It was at this time that 'Planned Maintenance' had just been introduced. We had not been properly briefed about the concept of this 'management technique'. At first it seemed like a lot of bullshit. It involved aircraft coming in for forty-hour inspections on a fixed rota, the object being to spread the maintenance work evenly, thus maximising the effectiveness of the maintenance ground staff.

Unfortunately we could not see the logic of having to put an aircraft in for maintenance when the sun was shining and we were doing our utmost to get as many aircraft into the air as possible. In fact, of course, this technique gave us a better rate of serviceability.

The air war had reached a stage when not only was the bombing campaign being stepped up, but aircrew losses were increasing. Consequently squadrons were screaming out for replacements, at the same time as new squadrons were being formed. This imposed a rigid discipline on flight programmes as well as on ground training coordination. My work was cut out preparing schedules and endeavouring to keep trainees on their toes.

With the onset of winter there were days on end when the weather clamped down, making flying impossible. One very foggy day the station commander thought it would be a good opportunity to have a full inspection parade. There were not many occasions when it was possible to have a full turn-out. The CO would take the salute at the watch tower, and I was detailed to be Officer in Charge.

The parade assembled on the main runway. The intention was to march up the main runway, wheel left at the intersection and return on the perimeter track to pass the saluting base outside the watch tower. I gave the order: 'By the left...' I reached the intersection and by then the gap between myself and the second in command had increased, and with visibility down to about 5 yards my second i/c had lost sight of me. Moreover, he could not have heard my command 'Left, wheel' and marched straight ahead. I did not notice that there were no sounds of marching steps behind me, so I carried on – alone! Fortunately the CO had a sense of humour, and half an hour later the whole parade returned to the saluting base. At that time there was a famous Guinness advertisement on hoardings depicting a detachment of soldiers marching past an advert 'Guinness is good for you'. All the men looking 'eyes left' at the advert marched off on a fork road to the left, while the officer in charge went off to the right.

The weather during November continued to be a mixture, with fine sunny days, with early morning fog, alternating with cloud and rain. December improved but still with foggy mornings. I was becoming quite concerned that we were falling badly behind with training schedules, so we had to get airborne at every opportunity. On 13 December the sky was brilliant blue, but visibility on the ground was poor. It did not appear to me to be too bad, but I decided to go up and carry out a weather test. Rather than waste time to get a crew together, I would just do a quick 'circuit and bump' on my own, to see what it was like above.

Horizontal visibility was not good, but I decided to chance it. (This sounds like 'famous last words'.) No sooner was I airborne than the visibility of the ground was absolutely nil. There was only one thing for it, and that was to go straight into 'timed circuit' and put my Link training to the test. As it happened, I had taken a Wellington III, which had not been fitted with standard beam-approach equipment. I had to rely on my Link training experience.

Having had plenty of practice doing timed circuits on the Link, I felt completely confident in my ability to cope. Now this was the time to prove it. Maintaining constant speed, rate of climb and direction, and carrying out a steady 'rate one' turn, I got round to the approach and lined up on the runway, still not visible. All this time I had not had sight of the ground. Easing back on the throttle and maintaining a steady rate of descent I felt quite happy I would be directly in line with the runway. As I crossed the threshold I found I was about 100 feet to the right of the runway. I could have side-slipped and brought her down without difficulty, but I decided to go round again, make another attempt and do it properly next time. I realised that I had not allowed sufficient compensation for the Giro compass processing. So I should allow a bit more, next time. I crossed the 'threshold' on the second attempt, bang over the end of the runway, throttled back and touched down. Once again I was thankful for all the training I had had. There can be little doubt that I owe my life to the high standard of training I had received. Primarily, of course, the object of flying safety is to avoid getting into difficult situations in the first place.

Most of our chaps did not like the job of being an instructor on an

OTU. I suppose one has to have a special aptitude to be an instructor. Like many others, I would dearly have liked to get back on to a Lancaster squadron. But I had already done two tours, so there was not much hope of that. Instead, at the end of January 1944 I was posted to India. And that is another story.

9. Overseas Again

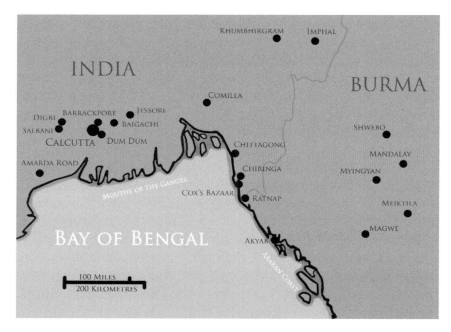

Through the normal progress of events in the Royal Air Force, one fully expected to get posted to the Far East at some time or other. No one ever relished the thought; from reports from chaps who had already been there and returned, it conjured up dire visions of heat, dust, sweat, malaria, fever and thirst. So when my posting came through, it was not entirely a surprise. The really hard part was telling my wife, Marie.

She had never been the clinging type, and never once betrayed her anxiety when I was on ops. Coping on her own with two small children, with all the wartime privations, never seemed to deter her, or at least she never showed it. However, being away from each other for three years was not a prospect we relished.

We had just enjoyed Christmas 1943 together in our new home in Manchester when I returned to No. 82 OTU at RAF Ossington. I reported back to my unit to be told I was being posted overseas! In no time I was told to report to sick quarters for the usual injections.

As soon as the CO informed me that embarkation leave was with effect from 30 January, that was the signal for the usual farewell piss-up on the Saturday. With very mixed feelings next morning I set off for Southport, where Marie and the two children had been staying at her parents' home. Anne was just coming up to her second birthday, and John was just a year younger. I received a telegram to report to No. 5 PDC at Blackpool. At last, after 'pissing around' for a fortnight between Blackpool and Southport, I got orders to report to Liverpool for embarkation. I boarded the SS *Orontes* on the 19th. We waited out in the Mersey for the convoy to assemble, eventually sailing on Monday, 21 February. The voyage passed without event.

By May 1942 the situation for the Allies in the Far East was precarious, to say the least. Following the attack on Pearl Harbor in December 1941, the Japanese had eliminated Allied influence in Indo-China and were poised, so the Allies thought, to attack India. As the official history recorded: 'On the Allied side of the front line, India was unprepared and ill-equipped for war and the air forces, now the first line of defence, were in a parlous state.'

When the RAF pulled out of Burma in May 1942 and joined the minute air force in India, there were on paper about fourteen squadrons, most of them battle weary and sadly depleted. Many had no aircraft at all while others were equipped with obsolescent types with few reserves behind them.

Over the course of the next year and a half 'seeds had to be sewn in virgin earth and many trials and tribulations experienced before a harvest was reaped'. One of the critical factors in the fight against the Japanese in Burma was clearly going to be air supply to the troops fighting on the ground, amid the 'inhospitable nature of the wilderness, which formed the battleground on the Burma front'.

'Apart from certain lines of communication which did not even join together to make access from one end of the country to the other, transport facilities were dated – if not primitive. Burma was still the land of the bullock cart and the sampan. Wide tracts of country were covered by thickly grown almost impenetrable stretches of palm and jungle wood, and there were fair-weather roads which disappeared under water during the months of the monsoon.'

The campaigns in Burma relied upon supplies ferried in by air. In line with the growth in air supply capabilities came the demand for fighter aircraft that could protect the transport aircraft and the logistical infrastructure from enemy air attack.

By mid-1944 it was essential to the Allies to maintain the serviceability and availability of aircraft, exploiting this hard-won air superiority. When Richard Pinkham arrived in India in March 1944, he was handed the responsibility of ensuring Allied aerial front-line strength, applying his experience to the understanding of aircraft accidents and then taking the necessary remedial measures.

We docked at Bombay a month later. No one seemed to know what to do with me! For ten days I enjoyed a life of leisure and luxury, swimming daily at the Breach Candy Club, while 'P' staff decided where to post me. After enjoying a cruise in the Mediterranean and Red Sea, I had had enough hanging around and was anxious to join a squadron, as I fully expected to do another tour of ops. Instead, I continued to spend every afternoon swimming and the evenings playing bridge at the Club. I reported daily to 'P' staff and was told to come back tomorrow. Eventually, on Thursday, 30 March, I was told to report to HQ ACSEA at Delhi. Here the situation was not much better: SNAFU (Situation Normal, All F***ed Up). In sheer frustration I demanded to see Air Commodore MacDonald, Air Officer Training. 'No there are no vacancies at Delhi. Go and report to Wing Commander Aiken.' He was not much more helpful. I suppose he thought the best way to get rid of me was to pass me on to another Command. So they decided to post me to Calcutta. The note in my diary is unprintable. I had heard that the river Hooghly was the 'arse-hole of the empire', and Calcutta was 100 miles up it! I saw Wing Commander Holme at Air Sea Rescue Service; the prospect hardly appealed to me, but at least I felt I was getting somewhere. He told me to report to No. 231 Group.

I boarded a train for Calcutta at 2055 hours, travelled all the next day, which was Good Friday, and arrived at Howrah station on Saturday, 1 April. It was over three months since I had been told I was being posted overseas, so I lost no more time in reporting to the 'P' staff officer. No. 231 Group HQ was located at Belvedere Palace, which had been commandeered by the Royal Air Force. I still had not finished with being pushed around, as I was then sent to the Senior Air Training Officer. 'No', he had no idea why I had been posted to No. 231 Group. 'No', they did not have any vacancies. 'No', he did not know what to do with me!

I reported to Wing Commander Cross, Group Training Officer. 'What do you want Squadron Leader?' (Normally you lose your acting rank when posted overseas, but I still had my stripes.)

'I've been told to report to you, Sir.'

'What's your name? We don't appear to have received a postagram for you.'

I reflected this was TARFU (Things Are Really F***ed Up).

'If you do not have a job for me Sir, does this mean I can return to UK?'

'I should not think so,' he replied, 'but I suppose we had better find something for you to do.'

The Group Training Officer had a large office. It was a bright office, sparsely furnished with two desks and two chairs. There was a map of Bengal and Burma on a wall and the inevitable ceiling 'punka' turning slowly, keeping the room pleasantly cool. One of the desks was in the corner of the office, but the top was bare. He said, 'Look here, take these two files and let me have your comments.'

'What are they Sir?' I queried.

'Accident reports,' he replied. 'Presumably you have seen one before.'

I did indeed know what an accident report was. I had had enough experience making them out as flight commander at OTU. So I spent half an hour reading through them, and wrote a memo to the GTO with my comments.

'Fine,' he said. 'You are now Group Accidents Officer. We have a vacancy for a flight lieutenant "Training Officer", but you can fill the vacancy supernumerary, and retain your acting rank.'

This sounded like a great opportunity, but as I had not had any training for the job I was somewhat apprehensive of the prospect. Still 'press on regardless', I thought, although I never expected that two years later I would be appointed Chief Accidents Officer for the whole of South East Asia.

The loss of aircraft, either damaged or destroyed, but not due to enemy action, was the cause of the greatest concern. During a period of six months at the end of 1944 in the Royal Air Force operations in Bengal and Burma, 416 aircraft were damaged or destroyed. This represented a significant proportion of all losses, including those lost through enemy action (see Appendix 4).

Four hundred aircraft put out of action represented a very disturbing restriction on the Allies' capacity for assault on the enemy. At this time the enemy was in full retreat, but our forces needed the maximum hitting power to take full advantage of our initiative, and to maintain the impetus of the ground forces. Figures cannot convey the full magnitude of the loss to the Allies' hitting power, but 400 aircraft on one mission would have represented a formidable force.

The RAF had a maxim: 'Accidents do not happen, they are caused.' Most accidents were avoidable.

I was posted to No. 231 Group Calcutta in April 1944, where my terms of reference were 'to reduce the accident rate'. No. 231 Group was the Bomb Group operating Liberators and by comparison with other groups had a relatively low accident rate. In September 1944 I was posted to Command HQ, 3rd Tactical Air Force, which encompassed the whole of the operation Wings in Bengal and Burma. In December I was appointed Chief Accidents Investigation Officer.

Before it was possible to carry out appropriate preventative measures, it was first necessary to discover the causes of accidents, and to analyse the results. Parallel with this line of action, it was equally important to carry out a meticulous survey of all aspects of flying safety. While it was the duty of a commanding officer to ensure that all safety measures were implemented, it was also necessary for inspections to be carried out, in order to make recommendations for improving safety precautions generally.

I do not deal with the element of prevention in this account. Regular inspections of Wings revealed many examples of lack of diligence, sometimes amounting to flagrant disregard of basic principles of flying safety, often indifference and complacency and occasionally wanton disobedience of safety regulations. It was the responsibility of the Accidents Officer to advise commanding officers of any such breaches and to make recommendations for improving flying safety.

After two years of concentrated effort, the accident rate for Bengal and Burma was virtually halved. The following account of investigations into flying accidents can represent only part of the story. It is based entirely on notes recorded in my diary, and records of statistics, but despite the lapse of sixty years the recollection of these events remains for ever fresh in my memory.

I managed to acquire manuals on 'Accidents Prevention' and 'Air Accidents Investigation', and I set about swotting up. I had no idea what the duties of a Group Accidents Officer might be, nor was I given any terms of reference or job specification. So it was virtually up to me to determine my own objectives and duties. I soon discovered what these should be, as it was not long before accident report files were coming in at an alarming rate. Alarming, not because I thought I might not cope, but because there were so many accidents.

No. 231 Group was the bomber group, operating with eight squadrons of Liberators plus a Conversion Unit, and a Communication flight. There were thirty-two crashes in three months on the Liberator squadrons. No. 232 Group was operating with seven Dakota squadrons. In the same period there were forty-nine accidents with Dakotas, and the Dakota was supposed to be one of the safest aircraft in the world.

I could see there was a mammoth task ahead of me and I was certainly going to be kept busy. It was not long before I was thrown in at the deep end. A Liberator had crashed at Jessore, which required a full investigation. Wing Commander Cross and I set off to the scene of the crash some 70 miles north-east of Calcutta. Although we were able to complete the task in two days, the result of this investigation was inconclusive.

It was not always possible to arrive at a positive result of an investigation, either because the evidence was insufficient, or because we lacked the technical resources to examine components that had failed. As a consequence of this accident, I set up an Accidents Committee at all Wings, the object being to review all aspects of flying safety and to ensure that all possible precautions were taken. Records were to be kept of all accidents, and analysed under type of accident.

The analysis would highlight types of accidents that were most prevalent, and enable us to concentrate on taking appropriate action to prevent recurrence of similar types of accident.

I was posted to HQ 3rd Tactical Air Force at Comilla (186 miles east of Calcutta) on 9 September 1944, with the acting rank of Wing Commander, responsible for the RAF and RIAF squadrons in Bengal and Burma, and was appointed Permanent President of Courts of Inquiry. Promotion was confirmed on 1 October. Then, on 23 December 1944, I was posted to HQ Eastern Air Command Barrackpore (10 miles north of Calcutta) as Chief Accidents Investigator, where we operated in close liaison with the USAAF.

Over the course of the next eight months Richard was to be involved in
numerous investigations into accidents. He did not record in detail the
results of all the investigations, hence not all the inquiries in which he was
involved are included in the following pages; however, he describes some
of the more interesting cases, with the occasional anecdote thrown in.

Chiringa – Beaufighter – 19 December 1944

I was able to pick up a Hurricane at Baigachi after having flown from
Dum Dum in a Tiger Moth. Speed is essential to get to the site of the
crash, so I was given 'top priority' to commandeer whatever aircraft was
available.

This Beaufighter had crashed 'conveniently' at the end of the runway
and had burnt out. There appeared to be little prospect of finding any
clues that would lead to solving the problem. It is, however, quite
surprising what can be discovered to provide a vital clue, even when the
wreckage is badly burnt.

The first principle to be observed in investigation is to approach it with
a completely open mind. There must be no preconceptions, no jumping
to conclusions, and it is important to avoid following false clues.

As soon as possible, with the help of the station commander, anyone
who may have witnessed anything or who may have been involved with
the maintenance or servicing of the aircraft should be interviewed while
the event is still fresh in their minds. The flight commander will provide
evidence of the pilot's ability and competence.

The investigation will then examine the wreckage, noting the attitude
of the aircraft when it hit the ground. This will indicate whether the
aircraft was in the stalled position, whether it hit the ground in a shallow
glide or a steep dive, whether it hit one wing down. Was the wreckage
spread over a long distance? Is it possible to deduce if the aircraft was
'under control'? Did it stall? Was the aircraft under power or throttled
back? Was there any evidence of damage to nearby trees or buildings?

In this case the aircraft had been seen to take off normally, with both
engines under full power; flaps and undercarriage had been raised soon
after take-off. But it had climbed steeply to an almost vertical position
before flipping over.

The flight commander gave a very praiseworthy account of the pilot's
ability and reliability. No pilot, however mad, would have attempted
such a split-arse climb after take-off, and this pilot was much too
experienced and responsible to do that. There was nothing abnormal in

the Flight Authorisation book. It was a test flight. Checking the F.700 revealed that it had been in for servicing and had had the elevators replaced. The pilot had carried out the correct pre-flight drill, testing controls and witnessed by the NCO.

Evidence pointed to one thing: the aircraft had gone into an ever-increasing rate of climb, until it had been near vertical, and hanging on its props. Why? Had the pilot inadvertently wound the elevator trim backwards instead of forward? Surely such an experienced pilot could not have made such a mistake. Certainly, as soon as you become airborne, and have raised undercarriage and flaps, it is necessary to adjust the elevator trim. If the pilot had made a mistake and adjusted the trim back, he would have realised this and wound the trim control forward a bit.

Despite the burnt-out wreckage, it was possible to find the elevator trim indicator, and it was clearly in the fully forward position – not back. So had that been the case, the aircraft would have been in the nose-down attitude. It was apparent that, the more the aircraft nose came up, the more the pilot wound the trim control forward, until he was physically unable to push the stick forward. The more he wound the wheel forwards, the more the nose came up.

It was almost miraculous luck that we were able to trace the elevator trim control cables from the control in the cockpit to the elevator trim tabs and they were intact. It did not take long to discover that the cables had been crossed! Although the NCO had checked that the tabs were working, he had not realised that they were operating in reverse.

Barail Mountain Range – Nr Kumbhirgram – Mosquito – 14 January 1945

This aircraft crashed in an inaccessible location in mountain jungle. There was no possibility of getting to the crash site. I flew from Calcutta in a Hurricane, 400 miles without radio, just flying on DR. Fortunately there were a number of good easily identifiable landmarks of rivers and lakes.

A full Court of Inquiry was convened, but the result was inconclusive. A squadron leader, who had assisted the court, managed to rustle up a few cans of beer, and he entertained me to the best curry I have ever tasted. He was a personality of some reputation, especially among the ladies. He had had a minor accident with his Smith & Wesson, which he usually carried in his trouser pocket. One day he stubbed his toe against a stone, stumbled and the revolver went off. The bullet went through the end of his penis and through his leg! Fortunately the injured 'weapon' soon healed, and he became very popular with the nurses.

Ratnap – Thunderbolt (No. 258 Squadron) – 13–17 February 1945

There had been a number of Thunderbolts exploding over the target area. They were being used as dive-bombers and consequently the losses were put down to enemy action. That is, until one day a kite blew up over the target and other pilots who returned safely declared that there was no anti-aircraft fire in the area. The explosions did not look as though the aircraft had been hit by flak or small-arms fire; in that situation there would normally be a fire before the explosion. These aircraft 'blew up' in a massive ball of flame, which was typical of an explosion resulting from a fuel leak.

However, as the Thunderbolt tanks were self-sealing, that did not seem to be the likely explanation. Luck was on our side again when one pilot returned complaining that petrol fumes had been filling his cockpit. As soon as the pilot reported the incident, a signal was sent to 3rd TAF. I sent a signal back: 'Don't touch anything until I get there.' I always kept a spare razor and toothbrush at the office, so that I could set off without a moment's waste of time.

Whenever an aircraft that had been built in the USA was involved, we always informed my counterpart in the USAAF, and they would send a technical specialist officer to assist with the investigation. On this occasion I took a USAAF technical officer with me. We flew in the Proctor, a gentleman's aircraft – not as fast as the Hurricane, of course, but with a useful range. We landed at Cox's Bazaar, which is some 65 miles south of Chittagong on the Akyab coast, and about 250 miles across the Bay of Bengal. This American technical officer was greatly impressed with the Proctor.

'What speed does she do?' he enquired.

'140 knots,' I replied.

'Gee, you don't say. That's great! What range has she got?'

'At 140 knots, with a duration of three hours, about 420 miles.'

'Gee, you don't say. That's great! We don't have anything like that in the States!'

'Gee, you don't say,' I replied. I did not tell him I did not like the way her nose stuck up in front, necessitating pronounced zigzag taxying.

As soon as we arrived at Ratnap we went straight to the aircraft, to find a number of airmen and officers around it. They had already carried out a superficial inspection, but could find no evidence of a fuel leak.

'Right chaps,' I declared. 'We must strip the kite, bit by bit, and I want to watch closely as each bit is removed. We'll start with the fuel tank, as this is the most likely source where the leak could be coming from.' After examining the tank externally for possible damage from flak, but finding no sign of damage, we removed the inspection panel to examine the tank internally. Again there was no obvious sign of damage. 'Now let's remove the whole tank.' We started by removing four small bolts securing a flange to the steel bulkhead, which was connected to a pipe at the top of the tank. As the last bolt was removed I saw the tank drop – probably not more than 2 millimetres. So, as the tank was self-sealing rubber, the whole weight of the tank and fuel would have been suspended in that flange. While the aircraft was flying straight and level there would have been no problem, but in the dive the level of fuel in the tank would have gone over the position where the flange was connected, and a gap would have been caused by the weight of the fuel stretching the aperture at the top of the tank. Although the gap caused by the weight of the full tank would not have been very big, it would have been sufficient to allow fuel to pour out, straight onto the hot engine exhaust. That would have been enough to ignite the fuel and create a highly explosive condition.

Further examination revealed no other possible cause of fuel leak that could have resulted in an explosion. Command HQ was signalled to the effect that all Thunderbolt aircraft should be grounded and a thorough examination carried out of the fuel-tank flange attachment. Thunderbolts were restricted to 'normal' flying and should not be used as dive-bombers until suitable modifications could be carried out. After that no further reports were made of any Thunderbolt exploding over the target area. Nor were there any reports from pilots of fuel vapour in the cockpit.

Jessore – Liberator (KG925) – engine failure – 26 February 1945

It did not take long to find out that the cause of the engine failure was due to contaminated oil. The investigation focused on the storage and source of oil supplies. Jessore is 65 miles north-east of Calcutta, and my colleague Wing Commander Chabot was responsible for accidents west of the Brahmaputra River. (I was responsible for those east of the Brahmaputra.) I passed the investigation on to him.

Chabot ('Shabby' as we called him) was a man of 50, of stocky build, with a bald pate that glowed like a beacon. He never wore a hat and did not seem to be affected by the sun. He was, however, very much a law unto himself. He did it 'his way'. Although he was old enough to be my father, I just happened to have seniority, but with his total disregard for higher authority I just let him get on with it and do what he wanted to do.

I did, though, have a very high regard and admiration for him. He had been a fighter pilot in the first war, and was a pilot of very considerable experience. He would fly anything from a Tiger Moth to a Liberator. I thought at his great age he would have been past it, but not him. I said, 'Here, Shabby, this is something right up your street. Oil contamination!' I briefed him and almost before you could bat an eyelid he was off like a terrier after a rabbit. I did not see him for three weeks! The AOC Air Commodore Lord 'Paddy' Bandon sent for me. 'Where's Chabot?' he demanded.

'I haven't the slightest idea Sir.' I feebly replied. 'He is supposed to be carrying out an investigation for me, into the source of contamination of oil supplies.'

'You are the senior officer and should be in charge. Why don't you know where he is and what he is doing? Get him back here immediately and have him report to me as soon as he returns.'

I shot off a signal to Delhi (copy all Wings): 'Where is Wing Commander Chabot?' After three days he turned up. 'What's the flap?' he breezily enquired.

'The Old Man's after your guts! Where the hell have you been?'

'You know I was following the route of oil supplies, well that's just what I did.'

'Surely that did not take you nearly four weeks?'

'Well actually, old boy, I have been to Aberdan.'

'Like hell you have. That's in Persia,' I exclaimed.

'Well, I traced the supply first to a depot at Ranchi [about 250 miles west of Calcutta]. From there I went on to Bombay, and the supply route led to Aberdan. That's where the contamination occurred.'

'I'll believe you, but I doubt if the Old Man will.'

At any rate there were no further problems with Liberator engine failure through contaminated oil.

I returned to my office to find another urgent signal asking me to report to Faridpur to investigate a Dakota crash (2 March 1945). I had to travel by train, as no Communications flight aircraft was available. Only ox carts are a slower form of transport in Bengal. I returned to Jessore to complete the Court of Inquiry. After that I had dinner with a missionary and returned by train in the evening. 'If only I had my own aircraft.'

After completing an investigation into a Thunderbolt crash (Amarda Road, 21 March 1945), I returned to the Officers' Mess, where I had a couple of 'John Collins' with the station commander. The Wing had recently converted from Spitfire Vs to Thunderbolts, and the pilots had not got accustomed to the new type. The handling properties were entirely different from those of the Spitfire; consequently there were a number of accidents that were primarily due to lack of familiarisation on type. There were two accidents that were due to stalling on take-off, with fatal results. There were five accidents of overshooting on landing. There were more than eleven accidents due to engine failure in a period of six months. I stayed at Amarda Road for several days, finishing off Courts of Inquiry. By 26 March I was ready to return to HQ.

I had a meal in the evening, and the station commander joined me with a couple more 'John Collins'. During conversation the subject turned to my problem of getting around Bengal and Burma with very limited resources of Communications flight aircraft and the great need to get to the scene of a crash as quickly as possible. Communications flight aircraft were not always available. 'What I need', I told him, 'is an aircraft that could be available at all times.'

'That's no problem', he replied. 'I've got a couple of dozen Spits that are surplus to requirements. They are all "fives" and have been replaced by the Thunderbolts. You can have one of them if you like.'

I thought, 'He's taking the piss out of me!' Nothing further was said and I retired. Next morning I went to the Mess for breakfast. He saw me and said, 'See me in my office when you've finished breakfast.' I thought he wanted to discuss with me the findings of my investigations. So I quickly finished breakfast and made my way to his office.

'Come on then,' he cordially greeted me, 'let's go to dispersal and see if we can find a serviceable Spit for you.'

'What do you mean?' I blurted. 'I have never flown a Spit in my life. I'm a twin-engine bomber type.'

'Can you ride a bike?'

'Yes,' I replied.

'Well if you can ride a bike, you can fly a Spit; it's as easy as riding a bike.'

'You must be joking!'

'Come on you can cope.'

He picked out one that looked in reasonable condition. 'Let's have a look at this one.' We walked round doing a 'pre-flight' check. 'Now get in and get the feel of it. Check the controls. Now I'll explain the "tits" and "knobs". Throttle. Pitch control. Flaps. Undercarriage. Mixture. Trim. Nothing to it, old boy!' he reassured me. 'OK, let's see you have a bash.'

I secured the harness, pulled it in tight, plugged in the intercom, and called up Control. 'This is C – Charlie. OK for take-off?'

'C – Charlie. OK for take-off. 270 degrees. Wind 10 knots. All clear for take-off.'

This brought back memories of my first solo at Gatwick (except we did not have RT then). I locked the brakes 'on' and opened the throttle and checked the 'mag' switches. OK. Check pitch – fine. Check flaps, 15 degrees. Check for anything in the circuit. 'This is it,' I thought. 'Here goes.' Having been used to the Wimpey (that is, the Wellington), which was a bit sluggish and needed plenty of room for take-off, I was not prepared for what happened next. When you open the throttles on a Wimpey, you have to open up fairly quickly to get maximum thrust as soon as possible. What happened next took me completely by surprise. It seemed I had had some giant give me a hard slap on the back, and before I could say 'Jack...' I realised with some concern that I was already airborne!

The problem now was that I had to put the bugger down without pranging it. So I took her up to 10,000 feet and stooged around doing some gentle turns to get the feel of it. Then I thought, 'I'll try a steep turn', and nearly blacked out in the process. 'Gently boy. Don't overdo it.'

The station commander's voice rang in my ears, 'If you can ride a bike...'. He was right; this was a piece of cake. Now let's see what she is like in a loop – mad bugger that I am. No problem – child's play – like riding a bike! It had been a long time since I last did a loop. Then I thought 'I must try stalling her', pulled the stick right back, throttled back until the speed dropped off, and what happened was that the nose dropped gently and she recovered without dropping a wing!

Better get back now, and get the CO to pass me 'qualified on type'. I got back into the circuit and I remembered seeing how all the fighter boys used to do what I thought was a 'split-arse' approach. At least that is what it looked like. Then I made my approach. I could not see anything of the airfield for the bloody great nose stuck up in front of me. I realised then the reason for side-slipping on the approach was to get a clear view of the landing strip ahead. Straightening up over the end of the landing strip, I throttled back, eased the stick back, held off for a couple of seconds, and then was down, gentle as a feather – 'like riding a bike'. I taxied up to the Control, where the CO was waiting for me. 'Good show, old boy. You can take her away on one condition. Promise me you won't bend her, and bring her back when she is due for a forty-hour inspection.'

I could hardly believe I was now the proud possessor of my own Spitfire. I flew it many times during the next few months.

Chiringa – Beaufighter – 27 March 1945

There had been a number of engine failures on No. 211 Squadron, No. 901 Wing Chiringa. Other Beaufighter squadrons had also had engine failures. It was discovered that there was a particular idiosyncrasy of the Hercules engine when it was shut down. Oil would accumulate in the lower cylinders. To prevent this, it was found that turning the propeller by hand after the engine had been stopped, so that the engine could make four complete revolutions, cleared the lower cylinders.

Baigachi – Spitfire investigation (MY411) – 6–8 April 1945

This was a particularly nasty accident. The Spitfire went into the ground in an almost vertical dive. The engine had buried itself about 30 feet into the ground. There was nothing that could be solved from the wreckage. There had been no witnesses to see the aircraft go in.

There had been no R/T contact. Weather conditions had been good. The F.700 did not reveal any technical problems. There was a remote chance that it could have been caused by a bird strike. It was one of those accidents that would always remain a mystery.

I returned to Comilla on 24 April. My assistant greeted me, telling me that the SASO wanted to see me. 'What's the Old Man want?' I enquired. Word had got round that I was in possession of my 'personal' Spitfire. 'I suppose I shall be for the high jump!' I thought. 'No doubt I shall soon find out.' Air Commodore 'Paddy' Bandon was a very popular officer, a really 'good type' you would say, sometimes known as the 'Abandoned Earl'.

'What's this I hear, Wing Commander? You have acquired your own personal Spitfire?'

'Well. It's like this Sir, I needed something to get me around with the minimum of delay, so that I could get to the scene of a crash as quickly as possible. A very kind Group Captain said he had several spare kites, and would I like one. I could hardly refuse such a kind offer!'

'That's all very well, but it is just not allowed in AM Regulations. We cannot have officers running around in their "own" aircraft. It is just not on, you know! Take it back where it belongs!'

'Yes Sir.' I complied.

It had been fun while it lasted. I could get to Kumbhirgram, a distance of about 400 miles, in one hour thirty minutes, whereas it would have taken twice as long in the Proctor.

It was not long after that, however, that I was posted to HQ Eastern Air Command at Barrackpore, to take up the post as Chief Accidents Officer. I don't think 'Paddy' Bandon could have been too upset with me after all.

10. Chief Accidents Officer

Ranchi – Mosquito (HR628, No. 684 Squadron) investigation – 18 May 1945

I now had only aircraft from Communications flight available to use – and as a passenger! There was not always an aircraft immediately available, which I found most frustrating. By the time I reached Ranchi I was feeling bad, with my sinuses giving me a lot of pain and causing bad headaches. However, I had to press on.

A Mosquito engaged in practising low-level attacks on the bombing range had crashed on the range. There had been some misgivings about operating Mosquitoes in the extremely humid conditions in that part of the world. The rumour had immediately spread around that the aircraft had 'broken up' because of humidity, causing failure of the laminated main spar. But, as pointed out before, it was very wrong to jump to conclusions before any investigation had even begun.

As there was some suspicion that the main spar lamination was defective, I examined this closely first. There was absolutely no sign of the laminations separating. I had the main spar taken back to the Maintenance Unit for closer examination, but my own finding was confirmed.

My sinuses were beginning to make me feel rotten, but I had to get on with examination of all the wreckage. This was spread back over 3 miles from the point of impact. Together with my team, we traced the trail of wreckage back to the location of the first piece of wreckage. We made a careful note of where each piece of wreckage was found. We eventually came across the starboard tail plane, in which there was a very obvious deep indentation on the leading edge, where something had evidently hit it. The tail plane had sheared off with the impact; as a consequence the aircraft would have gone out of control and crashed. A closer inspection of the root of the tail plane indicated that the break was 'backwards' and not 'upwards'. The leading edge of the tail plane spar showed a typical 'tension' break, and the rear edge of the spar indicated a typical 'compression' break. Something had evidently hit the tail place with considerable force. The indentation was 2 inches wide and about 1 inch deep.

We had to discover what had hit the leading edge of the tail plane. Paint deposits in the indentation were not paint from the tail plane itself. Clearly some tubular part had struck it.

By now I was feeling very bad, with severe sinus pain and headache. I had to report sick. I gave instruction to the senior NCO to have all the wreckage gathered up and laid out on the ground like a giant jigsaw puzzle, so that we could check up any component that might have broken off and struck the tail plane. I was too ill to carry on and reported to the unit MO and admitted to sick quarters. I had also developed severe tonsillitis and was in a shocking state. I remained in sick quarters for a whole week, but by 27 May I was sufficiently recovered to continue the investigation. I returned to the bombing range but was unable to make satisfactory progress. The NCO and his team of airmen and Indian helpers had collected all the wreckage they could find, and laid it out on the ground like a giant jigsaw, as I had instructed. Then a tubular strut with a diameter similar to the indentation of the tail plane was discovered. Paint deposits that matched the paint on the tail plane were also identified. There could be no doubt that the damage to the tail plane had been caused by this strut.

The location of the strut was the first bit of wreckage in line with the trail of wreckage, and clearly had broken off, then fallen after hitting the tail plane. This was in my opinion the secondary cause of the accident, but we still had to determine the primary cause, which was why the strut had broken off in the first place. The wreckage had been spread over too wide an area to discover the vital missing part, to determine why the strut had broken off. There was, however, sufficient evidence to justify having all aircraft thoroughly examined to discover if there was an inherent defect in the fixings. This was a most unsatisfactory and inconclusive result to the investigation.

HQ Eastern Air Command – Calcutta

I returned to HQ to discover a major flap on. The Chief Technical Officer wanted to ground all Mosquitoes. I could not see the justification for all this, but the decision was entirely out of my jurisdiction. I made my report on my findings, but it was up to the CTO to decide on the safety of continuing to operate Mosquitoes.

There had been two squadrons of Mosquitoes on photographic reconnaissance for three years, operating in extreme temperatures and humidity, without a single instance of the main spar failure. Subsequent inspection of all main spars on these two squadrons revealed 'no defect in the main spar laminations'. However, No. 45 Squadron and No. 82 Squadron, which were operating on low-level attack bombing and strafing, were grounded. It was proposed to re-equip these two squadrons with Vengeance aircraft. The pilots were horrified at the prospect; without exception they would all have preferred to continue on Mosquitoes instead of Vengeances.

By now the whole issue had gone back to the Air Ministry, and Geoffrey de Havilland came out personally to take part in the investigation. In the three months that the two squadrons had been operating on bombing, one Mosquito had been involved in a crash because of 'airframe' failure. There was a strong faction among technical staff at HQ that was advocating withdrawing Mosquitoes from operational flying in Burma. I was severely castigated by the Chief Technical Officer at Command HQ for my findings as a result of my investigation. He said I was doing the Royal Air Force a 'grave disservice'. Whatever he may have thought of my opinion, others must have had more regard for my competence, as it was not long before I was promoted to Chief Accidents Officer for the whole of South East Asia Command, Kandy, Ceylon.

Digri – Liberator investigation – 8 June 1945

Nothing is more irresponsible than speculating on the cause of an accident before all the facts are known. To be a good accidents investigator, it is essential to exercise rigid self-discipline to approach the investigation, right from the start, with a completely open mind. A typical example of this was the Liberator that crashed after a long-range flight back to Digri.

The aircraft had been on a long-range 'dropping' mission to Saigon, a round trip of 2,000 miles. With four overload fuel tanks, this would have been well within the range of this aircraft. In the event of possible fuel shortage, the aircraft could have landed at the advance base of Jessore, some 200 miles east of Digri. This sortie had been done many times before, but in the event of strong head winds the pilot was briefed to land at Jessore.

On the return flight the aircraft had passed over the advance airfield and the pilot had decided to attempt to get back to base. The crew were under the impression that there was still sufficient fuel in the reserve tank. Shortly after passing Jessore, the flight engineer switched over to the tank that he believed was still in reserve. Almost immediately all four engines cut in succession. The captain gave the order to bale out. The aircraft crashed in open country and the crew were safe.

The crew were interrogated immediately but had already got their story: 'the fuel cock to the reserve tank was u/s'. They claimed the flight engineer had been unable to switch over to the reserve tank.

Although the aircraft was extensively damaged, there had been no fire. On inspection, the tanks were all found to be empty. The crew were adamant that the fuel cock was u/s. Despite the extreme damage to the aircraft, it was necessary to recover the fuel cocks, which were retrieved. They were sent to the Maintenance Unit, where they were set up on a jig and tested, and found to be still in good working order.

The flight log was checked and the times when the fuel cocks had been changed over had been recorded. It was evident that they were still some considerable distance from the advance airfield when the last tanks had been switched over, but the flight Eengineer had estimated that there would have been enough fuel to get back to their home base.

Out there no one relished the idea of landing away from home base, and finding themselves in an advance airfield with minimum facilities. So, if there was half a chance of making it back to home base, with a good meal and a decent kip, they would chance it. Famous last words!

Mayu Peninsular – Liberator (KH316) – 29 June 1945

I received an urgent signal to proceed to Akyab at the mouth of the Kaladar River, just south of the Bengal/Burma border, 375 miles south-east of Calcutta. A Liberator had crashed into the mountain on the Mayu Peninsula on the Arakan coast.

The ridge of the mountain is about 1,100 feet above sea level, rising steeply, with the Mayu River on the east and the Bay of Bengal on the west. The Liberator had flown straight into the top of the mountain. Another couple of hundred feet and it would have cleared the mountain.

There was only one way to get to the scene of the crash and that was by the boat up the Mayu River. I spent the afternoon organising a team of fitters, armourers and an Air Sea Rescue unit to provide a launch to make the trip up the Mayu. There was no way of knowing what to expect, nor how long the investigation would be likely to take; so one had to be prepared for any eventuality. We had to be prepared to make our way through jungle, up the side of a steep mountain ridge: 1,100 feet above sea level may not be very high, but when one has not been trained for such conditions it is a very different matter. To make things really difficult, it was raining as only it can in Burma.

We set off at daylight the next day; there were about a dozen blokes in the team, including the launch crew. The ASR launch was a very sturdy craft, with two Merlin engines; it was about 60 feet long and used to setting out in heavy seas. We came round the head of the peninsular at the mouth of the river and as we crossed the bar we were met with huge rolling breakers, which tossed our craft about like a toy. We set course about 300 degrees for about 10 miles, being buffeted until we turned into the mouth of the Mayu River, where we experienced the same conditions, only this time we had the breakers following us. Every now and again the screws would come out of the water as we hit the crest of the wave and the engines would race like mad.

I thought, 'Well if this is "life on the ocean wave", I am very glad I am in the Royal Air Force!' Once we were in the Mayu River it was a relief to be in calmer waters. We sailed upstream about 20 miles before pulling into a sheltered creek. From here we had to make our way through thick jungle. We waded across a wadi and then started to climb up the steep side of the ridge. The thought passed through my mind: 'This is the sort of conditions that the poor bloody Army has to cope with all the time. Thank God I am not in the Army!' To add to our discomfort the rain was coming down in solid sheets and it was bloody cold.

We eventually reached the site of the crash. The bodies of the crew had already been moved. The Liberator had been on a bombing mission in Saigon, so before I could start on my work the armourers had to remove the guns and ammunition. Fortunately there were no bombs left in the aircraft, and most of the fuel had been used, so I could get on with my job inspecting the remains of the aircraft.

If the aircraft had totally run out of fuel, the propeller blades would have bent back, whereas if the engines were still under power, the propellers would have been bent sideways, which is how they were found. It was safe to conclude that there had not been engine failure; nor had the aircraft run out of fuel. In that event this would undoubtedly have resulted in a mayday call, which would almost certainly have been picked up. The Met Office reported that the weather conditions at the time of the crash had been atrocious. Having been on a long bombing mission, the pilot would not have been sure of his position; in fact he was well off course. The pilot would have been aiming to let down below the cloud, assuming that by that time he would be well over the sea and that it would be safe to descend below cloud.

Our job was done, so we made our way back to the boat. All the time it had been raining heavily, so we were soaked and cold – bloody cold. But we still had the return trip to face, including getting back across the bars at the mouth of the Mayu and Kaladar rivers. We were again subjected to the rigours of the sea. Waves kept breaking over the launch, and I just could not believe that it could stay afloat in those conditions. All the time we were getting wetter and colder.

It was with great relief that we saw the dock lights ahead, as by then it was already quite dark. We moored alongside and all the blokes bundled into a wagon to take us back to the RAF unit. As soon as we got into the office I phoned the MO, told him how perished and frozen the chaps all were, and requested a rum ration for everyone. The MO gave the medical orderly authority to issue us all with a tot of rum. His hand must have slipped when he poured out my shot, as he half filled a tumbler. I had never before had any real Navy rum, but, having been used to drinking my whisky straight, I knocked back a good half of what was in the tumbler. For a moment I thought I was going to explode.

I made sure that the chaps all got a good hot meal and I returned to the Officers' Mess. I had a good clean-up and changed into dry clothes. After I had eaten, I discovered a piss-up well in progress in the Officers' Club, where I had a couple of 'John Collins', and by that time the rum and 'John Collins' were having their effect. Needless to say I had one hell of a hangover next morning, but recovered sufficiently to get the next Communications flight Dakota back to Dum Dum (Calcutta).

The next day, Tuesday, I flew to Salbani, which was the Liberators' base, to conduct a full Court of Inquiry. I returned to HQ on Thursday, 5 July, having been away a whole week. I was glad to get back and have a good clean-up, a hot bath and a good kip. By the Saturday my sinus was giving me trouble again, so I reported to the MO on the Sunday, but I got another urgent call to go to Kinmagoan to do another Mosquito investigation. However, a full Court of Inquiry was required.

Kinmagoan – Mosquito (RF600 No. 110 Squadron, crashed on 3 July) – Court of Inquiry – 8 July 1945

Kinmagoan is just north of Myingyan, which is 457 miles east of Calcutta. The problem that I was always faced with since I had been deprived of my 'private' Spitfire was that I had to depend on Communications flight aircraft, which invariably were not scheduled to suit my convenience. So I had a couple of days off while I waited for an aircraft. The aircraft had hit a bump on the airfield while taking off, had became airborne prematurely and stalled.

This part of Burma had seen some of the worst fighting of the whole war. First it had been overrun by the Japs, and then they had been pushed back fighting a desperate rearguard action. Every inch of ground had been fought for, and what the Japs had not destroyed, we had finished off. I never saw such utter devastation: whole villages and towns had been totally flattened. Even the beautiful pagodas, and there were many, had all been badly damaged.

Yamethin – Thunderbolt (KL260, No. 34 Squadron) – Investigation – 12 July 1945

I flew to Meiktila, where I had to borrow a Jeep to get to the scene of the crash. By the time I reached the site, a dozen or so USAAF personnel were already on the scene. Typically no one appeared to be in charge, and no one seemed to have any idea what accidents procedure should be initiated. Immediate inspection of the wreckage revealed that one of the propeller blades was missing.

Closer examination of the propeller blade root showed typical concentric semi-circles of a 'crystal' formation on the surface, which were recognisable signs of metal fatigue. This was the only instance recorded in this theatre of operations of a propeller blade breaking off. One bright US Technical Officer came up with a great idea. 'We must send it back to base Maintenance Unit to apply the "Magnaflux test"!' He probably impressed some with his technical expertise, but I pointed out that the 'Magnaflux' test was used to detect cracks in metal, which are not normally visible to the eye, but which can be an incipient defect leading to total breakage. As the propeller blade had broken off, it was a bit too late to detect a crack.

A search party set off to find the missing propeller blade. It was recovered a few miles away. The resultant vibration of the engine, set up when the blade broke off, would have made it impossible for the pilot to control the aircraft, and he was also unable to bale out. A report was immediately signalled to Air Command, and all Thunderbolts were grounded until a thorough inspection had been carried out of all propeller blade roots for incipient fatigue cracks.

I had been out since early morning and returned to base at 1700 hours. The first thing I did was to strip off and swim in the nearby lake – taking a chance there were no QA nurses in the near vicinity. Later I did meet a couple of them in the Mess, and they invited me to go with them for another swim – but the rest of this episode is best left to the imagination.

Yamethin – Dakota (KN218, No. 117 Squadron) – Investigation – 15 July 1945

I received a signal that a Dakota had crashed about 80 miles south-west of a spot in the jungle, several miles north-west of Magwe. There was no point in returning to HQ, so I got the Unit Transport Officer to fix me up with a Jeep and an LAC driver. We loaded up with a good supply of rations; we took a Tommy gun for the LAC, and I always carried a Smith & Wesson 38.

There was no way of knowing how long an investigation might take, so, as I never knew how long we were likely to be away, I had to be prepared for all eventualities. In fact we were away for two whole days, but it took another two days to complete the Court of Inquiry.

We set off at first light and reached Magwe at 1500 hours. The direct route would have been no more than 80 miles, but, with no good roads, we had to take a long detour, covering two sides of a triangle and a distance of nearly 150 miles. This would not have taken too long but for the fact that the road was full of shell holes all the way. Progress was painfully slow, and we took turns to drive. We had to cross two high ridges, with steep hills. It was wild and desolate country and the journey took six hours. We saw very little sign of life, so we would have been in trouble if we had had a breakdown.

We reached the Irrawady, where we had to make a crossing somehow. I contacted an Army detachment at Magwe and found the CO, Lieutenant Colonel Malloy, to be most helpful. However, there was no way I could take the Jeep over the river, so I left my driver with the Jeep, and proceeded on my own. I had to make my way about 10 miles upriver to reach Salin to the west of the river. It was a very wide and fast-flowing river, and the only means available of getting across was by boat. I contacted a local boatman, who had a dug-out tree-trunk canoe. To my astonishment, this primitive form of transportation had the incongruous distinction of being propelled by an outboard motor.

The trip, while uneventful, was nevertheless a hair-raising experience. The sides of the canoe were no more than 3 or 4 inches above the water level. I sat very still. I thought, 'It's far safer flying over Germany!'

On reaching the west bank I was met by the local District Officer, U Chitt Pe. He had been contacted by Lieutenant Colonel Malloy and told to expect me. He too had a Jeep, and he took me to his home at Salin, where I met his charming wife and delightful little daughter. They gave me a meal and a bed. They were so charming and hospitable. Next morning we set off in his Jeep at 0700 hours, and he took with us his personal cook servant, who I found out later was to provide the most unexpected and pleasant surprise.

We soon reached a small farmstead, which was at the end of a cart track, and as far as the Jeep could go. We left the Jeep with the cook servant at the farm. U Chit Pe and the farmer accompanied me in the farmer's bullock cart, through scrubland as far as the cart could go. From there on it was foot slogging through dense undergrowth. Progress was slow. The going was getting rougher, and the sun getting hotter. Eventually we reached the site of the crash about 1000 hours.

The Dakota was broken up. It looked as if a giant had torn its wings off like tearing the wings off a butterfly. One wing was lying a considerable distance from the main wreckage, which had fallen almost straight down. The tops of trees close to the wreckage had been broken off where the aircraft had struck them. The main part of the fuselage and one wing were in a fairly compact area; only trees close to the crash were damaged. On examining the wing root and the wing that had been torn off, it was easy to see that the wing had been torn off literally in an upward direction.

Checking with the Met Office revealed the weather conditions at the time: the aircraft had been flying in violent cumulo-nimbus cloud. The Met Officer estimated the upwards currents would have been up to 100 miles per hour. Even the Dakota, which had a remarkably low accident rate and was built to withstand enormous stresses and strains, could not cope with the violent up-current. I was satisfied beyond all reasonable doubt as to the cause of the accident. The primary cause was the adverse conditions.

However, my adventure was not over. By now it was high noon and I was beginning to feel the effect of the heat. My water bottle had long since been empty, and I began to feel the effect of heat stroke. U Chit Pe put me on the farmer's cart and tried to make me as comfortable as possible, but every time the wheels went over a bump it felt as though someone was hitting me on the head with a mallet. We got back to the farm, where he had left his servant, and after a good shower and a drink of 'pinika pani' I soon recovered. But a big surprise was to come. It was by now about 1500 hours and we had been away for about eight hours. There in the farmyard were some upturned crates and boxes and I was bid to sit down. The cook then produced a meal that could have done justice to any good-class restaurant. We started with soup, followed by roast chicken and vegetables, pineapple and cream, to finish off with coffee. I thought I must have still been delirious from heat stroke, but it was real enough. All round us we were watched by little children and goats, while we tucked into this delicious meal. How had the cook known what time we would be back, and had everything just ready immediately we returned? No meal has ever tasted better in my life; it was just one of the most memorable meals of a lifetime.

There was no time to relax, however, and we had to get on our way, as it was getting late. We got back to Salin about 2030 hours, and again I spent the night as the guest of U Chit Pe and his wife. Next morning he took me back to the dug-out canoe, the trip downstream was soon accomplished and I got back to Magwe about 1130 hours, where my driver was anxiously waiting for me. After a quick lunch we set off about 1300 hours.

Recalling that the journey had taken us on two dog-legs of at least 150 miles, covered with shell holes, I studied the map, and saw that there was a track taking a more direct route, which I estimated would have been about 80 miles. I decided to risk taking the direct route. The map clearly showed a road of some sort. To begin with the going was quite reasonable, but gradually conditions deteriorated, and eventually the 'road' became nothing more than a cart track. In true RAF tradition, 'per adua...', we decided there was no turning back. At least my driver agreed with me. 'Press on regardless.'

Inevitably we came to a wadi. The only way to cross would have been to ford, but there was no sign to indicate that a ford where it would have been safe to cross existed. So we drove along the side of the river bed, looking for somewhere that might appear to be a suitable place to cross. We had not gone far before we were well and truly stuck in the mud, quite unable to move forward or backward, even with the Jeep's four-wheel drive. Now what to do? We really were up s**t creek!

There was still plenty of daylight left, so we were not unduly concerned. We must be able to find someone with a bullock who could pull us out. I told my driver to remain with the Jeep, while I would set off on foot to find help. I advised him, 'Keep your gun at the ready, and don't be afraid to use it if threatened.' I set off on foot, with my hand on my revolver, likewise, just in case.

I carried on around a bend in the river, and walked for what seemed at least 3 or 4 miles, when I came upon a group of village huts. There were one or two people about, but as soon as they saw me they all scampered inside. 'Now what?' I asked myself. I walked into the village, which now appeared deserted. I just stood there, not daring to knock on a door, in case I got a hostile reception. Eventually curiosity got the better of them. First a few children popped their heads outside, and some then dared to venture out, followed by more and more adults.

Being unable to speak a word of Burmese, I had to resort to sign language. How do you let someone know, who does not understand your language, that your Jeep is stuck in the mud, and that you need help? Making sounds that were supposed to resemble a vehicle, and a sign that looks as if you cannot budge! But signs and sounds are not necessarily universal. Somehow I managed to convey the message that I needed help, after much agitated gesticulation. The idea gradually seemed to dawn on them, and as they began to realise my predicament, they all started laughing. There was a good deal of animation, which puzzled me, as they all suddenly disappeared into a hut. 'Well,' I thought, 'that's bloody useless. Now what?' But eventually they all came back – the whole village of men and boys of all ages carrying chains, ropes, planks of timber and, as it seemed to me, anything they could lay their hands on. They were all laughing their heads off at my embarrassment, although at the time my sense of humour had eluded me.

There must have been thirty or forty of them, as they proceeded to march in the direction of the source of my predicament. We came to a point on the river where it was necessary to cross, so I stopped to remove my boots and socks, and roll up my trousers. This enabled the bulk of the party to get ahead of me. As we rounded the bend in the river, my driver and the Jeep came into view. What he saw alarmed him. All he saw was a hoard of ruffians armed with staves and ropes, with me surrounded by them. His reaction naturally was 'My God! They've got the Wingco. Now they are coming to get me!' Remembering my advice, he raised his gun, but in the nick of time I called out that I was all right, and he was not to worry; they had come to help.

The head man of the village soon sized up the situation, and with one word from him the entire 'force' got round the Jeep and lifted it completely out of the mud and onto firm land. Were we relieved! But they were obviously due some show of appreciation for their help. With lively gesticulation they made it quite clear they wanted a ride on the Jeep – all forty of them at the same time. I managed to persuade them that the Jeep was hardly adequate to take them all at one time, but I managed to take eight or so at a time, drive them along a dry part of the river bed then come back for a further load, until they had all had a ride. This they really appreciated. After they had all been given a ride, I thought, 'What can I give them to show my gratitude?' Money would be useless, as I had only sterling, which would not have been any use to them. Then the idea struck me. We had a large tin of 'hard-tack' biscuits in our emergency rations.

There would have been about forty-eight hard-tack biscuits in the tin. I had never had occasion to eat one, so I had no idea what they were like. They were about 3 inches square, very hard and looked most unappetising, but they were loaded with nutrition. I opened the tin and dished them out so that they had about two each. If I had given them gold, I do not think they would have been more pleased. Now that I had made my gratitude understood, they stood back to let me proceed on our way, but not before one of the older men indicated that he wanted to come with us. At first I was a bit slow on the uptake, but my driver pointed out that he thought he wanted to show us the way. This was precisely what he intended. So we set off. He rode with us giving directions for at least 10 miles. How he expected to get back I do not know, but he insisted on staying with us until we were well on the right track.

By now it was getting late in the afternoon, and I could see we were not likely to make it back to base until well after dark. Although we were now back on a cart track, the way was through scrub and densely wooded land. The cart track had been worn to deep gullies by rain, so we had difficulty in avoiding the wheels getting into the ruts. However, we managed to keep going. It was very rough going indeed and had now become dark. Darkness falls suddenly in that part of the world.

We managed to keep going but frequently had to reverse when the ruts were so deep that it was impossible to go on. We were hemmed in on all sides by undergrowth and had no idea where we were, nor how far we still had to go, or even if we were going in the right direction. The journey was becoming something of a nightmare. I half expected to see the eyes of some wild animal reflecting in the headlights.

We had been going for about two hours in the dark, and I was wondering if we would ever reach civilisation. Suddenly we came to a tarmac road, and, as I was not sure where we were, I guessed we should turn right. The going was not easy, but in about half an hour we were able to see lights. (At that time Jap bombers were well out of range.) We eventually got back to Meiktila at 2130 hours. Eight and a half hours' driving in most difficult conditions. A total distance of 290 miles.

I stayed on at Meiktila for another day, to carry out further enquiries. The following day, 19 July, I conducted a full Court of Inquiry. I got in touch with an acquaintance, a Sister Rhona Black, who came with me for a swim, and then on to the Mess for dinner. I still had to hang around for the next two days waiting for an aircraft to take me to Chittagong. I was not that bothered, as it gave me the opportunity to see Rhona again.

On Sunday I managed to get a flight back to Chittagong, where there was a good ENSA show in the evening, followed by a party in the Mess.

On Monday, 23 July, I had to conduct a full Court of Inquiry. On the Tuesday, the station commander asked me to give a talk to pilots on flying safely. I returned by transport aircraft to Calcutta, getting back to my quarters at 1600 hours. As soon as I had got into some clean clothes I made straight for the swimming baths in Calcutta. Just as a matter of interest I weighed myself. I had lost 3lb during that fortnight – hardly surprising.

Thunderbolt (KJ167) – Court of Inquiry – 26 July 1945

No rest for the wicked; another Thunderbolt crash. The inquiry was fairly straightforward; the conclusion: 'Cause of Accident – Main tank vent pipe elbow joint rubber connection loose. Fuel vapour entered cockpit. Pilot force-landed safely.'

On returning from Chittagong I had been informed that the whole of Air Staff was to be transferred to Rangoon within ten days. All activities at Barrackpore ceased completely. We spent most of the time waiting for embarkation, swimming at the club, and dining and drinking in the evenings. This was an opportunity to pay a visit to Firpo's, the Grand, the Great Eastern and the Porto Rico Club.

We got embarkation orders to board the SS *Rajula* on Monday, 6 August, at 2030 hours. While awaiting boarding instructions, I started to develop severe sinus pains. As soon as I was on board I reported to the ship's MO. His treatment consisted of soaking a full length of gauze finger bandage in Ephedrine and Cocaine, which he proceeded to stuff right up my nostril. He told me to keep it there as long as I could. Feeling absolutely lousy, I went up on deck. Utterly fed-up, I stuck it out for a while, wandering about the deck, until eventually I could stand it no longer. I started to pull the bandage slowly out of my nostril. It was not long before I had attracted an audience. Like a magician I continued to pull the bandage out. It seemed endless. The looks on the faces of my audience were of utter disbelief.

On 10 August 1945 the Japs surrendered. We docked at Rangoon on VJ Day and I reported sick. The MO, Wing Commander Stidolph, had me admitted to sick quarters. I am not likely to forget that day. I was feeling absolutely terrible. While everyone was going wild celebrating the surrender, I felt more like dying. The next day I was transferred to No. 38 British General Hospital, where I was to spend a week.

The ward was full of patients, about twenty officers of all ranks. Slowly I responded to treatment. We were very well looked after, and well supplied with goodies and free cigarettes. I had never smoked before, but lying there gazing at the ceiling all day, with nothing better to do, I started smoking. In those days a cigarette was the first resort for any invalid. I did, however, have plenty of time to study all the other patients. After a few days I was able to take more notice of what was going on around me. I was particularly disgusted by the way some of the senior officers treated the nurses as if they were still on parade. 'Nurse! Bring me a bed-pan!' No 'please' or 'would you mind'. Fortunately the nurses knew how to handle them. In particular, Sister Margaret Lowery, the ward sister, impressed me with her calm dignified manner. She certainly knew how to put some of those 'brass hats' in their place. She was about 30, with a slim, slight build, dark hair and blue eyes. Athough I never saw her smile, she was always particularly kind to me.

After the fifth day I was feeling well enough to get up, but Sister Lowery was nowhere to be seen. I enquired where she was, and was told that she was sick. I decided that as she had been so kind to me the least I could do was to go and see her, and see if she needed cheering up. She was most appreciative, but I never saw her again. The next day I received a postagram to report to HQ South East Asia Air Command at Kandy, to take up the appointment as Chief Accidents Officer.

I boarded a Sunderland to take me from Rangoon to Ceylon. It gave me a real thrill to have the opportunity to be taken as a passenger. The only word adequately to describe this magnificent aircraft is 'grandeur'. We took off from the Syriam Air Base at 0700 hours and touched down after nine and a half hours' flying time at the Noggala Seaplane base at 1630 hours. We circled the lagoon at Noggala to behold a spectacular sight of more than a dozen white Sunderlands moored around the lagoon, looking like graceful swans.

I spent the night at a transit camp, and proceeded by road the following day to Colombo, where at 1800 hours I caught the Services train that was due to arrive at Kandy at 2230 hours.

The train was nearly full by the time I got on board; there was, however, just one seat vacant, next to an English girl. She had obviously been swimming, as her hair was lank and bedraggled. I asked if the seat was vacant, and she invited me to sit. It was a long journey and in that part of the world it gets dark after six, so we were unable to enjoy the scenery, and the time passed slowly. Conversation between us, even though it was sporadic, was easy. On arrival at Kandy station we boarded separate transport to our respective Messes and bade each other 'au revoir'.

After I had booked in and been allocated quarters I went to the Mess for a meal, where I met an old colleague who asked me if I would be going to the Officers' Mess party that evening. I told him I was feeling tired after so much travelling, and I planned to have an early night. It did not take much to persuade me to change my mind. I turned up at the dance, and, to my surprise and delight, almost the first person I met was the girl I had sat next to on the train the night before. A complete transformation had taken place. She was beautiful; her golden blonde hair was curled in the fashionable style of that period, almost shoulder length. She wore an off-the-shoulder close-fitting dress showing off a divine figure. Our eyes met and there was instant electricity between us.

For the next seven weeks, we were never out of each other's company. We dined at the Suisse Hotel and the Chungking Chinese Restaurant. We danced at the Officers' Club and the Queen's Hotel. We swam at Mount Lavinia. We stayed at the Galle Face Hotel. We went up to a hill station at Campala and swam in the ice-cold mountain pool. It was so good while it lasted.

I was brought back to my senses with a sharp jolt, when I received a letter from Marie, my wife. She had been unwell for some time and as a result her periods had stopped. I was very disturbed and worried.

I applied for compassionate leave. I had been away from her for virtually four years, and I knew that if I could get back to see her she would soon get better. However, no leave was granted, as all passages home were fully taken by either sick and wounded, time-expired, or due for release.

I went to see the Senior Personnel Officer, but he told me that no compassionate leave would be granted unless the wife was extremely ill and there was a chance of her dying. He told me that Group Captain Leonard Cheshire VC was in the same boat; his wife was ill and he could not get compassionate leave either, even for such an officer who had served his country so well. I was faced with the choice of taking my 'de-mob' and returning to the UK with the option of signing on for a further period, or of staying on in the East, where I had been promised a posting to Singapore with promotion.

It did not take long for me to make up my mind. Marie was more important to me than either the Royal Air Force or promotion. I spent the last evening with Ida at the Galle Face Hotel on Sunday, 14 October 1945. We said 'Good-bye' without tears or regrets. We had known that our affair was too good to last. Ida also knew that Marie was my only real love.

I set off from Colombo on 15 October, arriving at Bombay on the 21st. We embarked on the SS *Samaria* on the 27th. We docked at Liverpool on 14 November, and I made my way home as quickly as I could. I was glad I had made the right decision.

After the war Richard spent a further two years in the RAF Reserve, 'but they did not want me. They wanted younger men.' Richard went back into the family business, Pinkham Gloves, and ran a factory in Durham, over-seeing a considerable growth in the business. But it did not last. The market dried up, and one morning Richard turned up to work to meet the company receiver 'and that was that'. He then took a job with the Productivity Association as a Productivity Officer, advising companies on improving their manufacturing, but when the government withdrew support he looked else-where and joined the Milton Keynes Development Corporation, responsible for persuading industrialists to come to the rapidly growing town, where he remained until retirement.

Richard's first wife, Marie, died in 1982, and Richard remarried, to Loreen, in 2007, who had unknowingly played an important role in the war, with the 'boring' job of spending hour upon hour every day writing down the Morse intercepts of enemy signals, including those of the German High Command.

When asked how the war affected Richard, he states simply: 'I had a job to do and got on with it. I was not thinking of possible consequences. It never occurred to me that I might get killed. My motivation to join the RAF was to fly. I never stopped to consider whether or not it was morally right or wrong. I was in the Royal Air Force, I had a duty and I got on with it.' When asked why a specific Bomber Command medal was not awarded to all relevant aircrew at the end of the war, Richard responds: 'I didn't think about it. I did what I had to do to the best of my ability and I considered I was lucky to have survived.'

Appendix 1

Wing Commander Richard Pinkham DFC, Record of RAF Service

Unit		From	To
No. 19 E&R FTS	Gatwick	8 August 1939	1 September 1939
No. 19 E&R FTS	Fairoaks	1 September 1939	5 October 1939
No. 3 SFTS	South Cerney	24 October 1939	27 April 1940
No. 10 OTU	Abingdon	4 May 1940	29 June 1940
No. 77 Sqn	Driffield	30 June 1940	28 August 1940
No. 77 Sqn	Linton-on-Ouse	28 August 1940	5 October 1940
No. 77 Sqn	Topcliffe	5 October 1940	14 March 1941
No. 10 OTU	Abingdon	15 March 1941	3 November 1941
No. 1481 TT flt	Binbrook	4 November 1941	21 August 1942
No. 150 Sqn	Snaith	22 August 1942	24 September 1942
No. 1503 BAT flt	Holme	24 September 1942	29 September 1942
No. 150 Sqn	Snaith	30 September 1942	26 October 1942
No. 150 Sqn	Kirmington	27 October 1942	9 December 1942
No. 1 OADU	Portreath	10 December 1942	17 December 1942
No. 328 Wing	Blida, north-west Africa	18 December 1942	31 December 1942
No. 150 Sqn, No. 328 Wing	Blida	1 January 1943	15 April 1943
No. 1 PDC	West Kirby	2 May 1943	4 June 1943
No. 82 OTU	Ossington	5 June 1943	20 June 1943
FIS	Church Broughton	20 June 1943	25 June 1943
No. 82 OTU	Ossington	25 June 1943	14 August 1943
No. 82 OTU	Gamston	14 August 1943	January 1944
No. 5 PDC	Blackpool	9 February 1944	19 February 1944
No. 231 Group	Calcutta	20 March 1944	5 September 1944

Unit		From	To
HQ 3RD TAF	Comilla	5 September 1944	3 December 1944
HQ EAC	Calcutta	4 December 1944	6 August 1945
HQ Burma	Rangoon	10 August 1945	28 August 1945
HQ ACSEA	Kandy	28 August 1945	13 October 1945
No. 104 PDC	Blackpool	27 October 1945	18 November 1945
No. 274 MU	Swannington	4 February 1946	February 1947

Key

ACSEA . . . . Air Command South East Asia
BAT flt . . . . Blind/Beam Approach Training flight
EAC . . . . Eastern Air Command
E&R FTS . . . . Elementary & Reserve Flying Training School
FIS . . . . Fighter Instructors' School
MU . . . . Maintenance Unit
OADU . . . . Overseas Air Dispatch Unit
OTU . . . . Operational Training Unit
PDC . . . . Personnel Despatch Centre
SFTS . . . . Service Flying Training School
TAF . . . . Tactical Air Force
TT flt . . . . Target Towing flight

Appendix 2

Wing Commander Richard Pinkham DFC, Operational Sorties Credited

The following is a list of Richard's operational sorties as recorded in his logbook.

	Date	Aircraft	Position	Entry in logbook	Flight time
	No. 77 Squadron 1940				
1	2 July	Whitley V	Second pilot	Evere–Brussels	6.15
2	19 July	Whitley V	Second pilot	Bremen	6.25
3	21 July	Whitley V	Second pilot	Kassel	7.35
4	9 August	Whitley V	Second pilot	Mannheim, Mildenhall, Base	7.15
5	12 August	Whitley V	Second pilot	Heringen. Aluminium works	8.00
6	14 August	Whitley V	Second pilot	Bordeaux. Oil Plant tanks. Land at Harwell	7.55
7	18 August	Whitley V	Second pilot	Milan. Aircraft factory. Land at Abingdon	9.25
8	2 September	Whitley V	Second pilot	Frankfurt – Mission	8.05
9	8 September	Whitley V	Second pilot	Ostend. Struck by lightning	4.20
10	10 September	Whitley V	Second pilot	Search over North Sea	6.45
11	13 September	Whitley V	Second pilot	Calais	4.05
12	15 September	Whitley V	Second pilot	Ostend	4.00
13	22 September	Whitley V	Second pilot	Dresden. Land at Massingham	9.40
14	2 October	Whitley V	Pilot	Rotterdam. Bad weather	5.15
15	7 October	Whitley V	Pilot	Amsterdam. Successful	6.00
16	20 October	Whitley V	Pilot	Weseling (near Bonn). Target located	7.30
17	26 October	Whitley V	Pilot	Pölitz (near Stettin). Successful	10.15
18	29 October	Whitley V	Pilot	Magdeburg. Bad weather	7.45
19	5 November	Whitley V	Pilot	Turin. Unsuccessful	7.25

	Date	Aircraft	Position	Entry in logbook	Flight time
20	10 November	Whitley V	Pilot	Dresden. Successful	11.00
21	12 November	Whitley V	Pilot	Weseling. Successful	7.30
22	14 November	Whitley V	Pilot	Berlin. Successful	9.10
23	16 November	Whitley V	Pilot	Hamburg. Successful	9.40
24	3 December	Whitley V	Pilot	Mannheim. Target located	10.15
25	10 December	Whitley V	Pilot	Mannheim. Bad weather	8.00
26	15 December	Whitley V	Pilot	Magdeburg. Successful	10.10
27	21 December	Whitley V	Pilot	Merseburg. Target not located. Land at Yeadon	9.00
28	27 December	Whitley V	Pilot	Bordeaux. Successful. Return to Abingdon	9.00
	1941				
29	2 January	Whitley V	Pilot	Bremen. Successful	8.05
30	10 February	Whitley V	Pilot	Hanover. Successful	7.05
	1942				
	No. 1481 flight				
31	31 July	Whitley V	Pilot	Düsseldorf. Returned, turret u/s	3.40
	No. 150 Squadron				
32	28 August	Wellington III	Co-pilot	Operations to Saarbrücken. Target located. Land at Bassingbourn	6.05
33	8 September	Wellington III	Pilot	Operations on Frankfurt. Successful. Emergency landing at Manston	5.15
34	10 September	Wellington III	Pilot	Operations on Düsseldorf. Successful	4.55
35	14 September	Wellington III	Pilot	Operations on Bremen. Successful. Land at Binbrook	4.50
36	16 September	Wellington III	Pilot	Operations on Essen. Successful. Land at Marham	5.10
37	18 September	Wellington III	Pilot	Mine-laying off Lorient. Successful	5.40
38	19 September	Wellington III	Pilot	Operations on Saarbrücken. Target located	6.50
39	10 October	Wellington III	Pilot	Mine-laying off Saint-Nazaire. Successful	6.45
40	22 October	Wellington III	Pilot	Operations on Ruhr. Successful	4.40
41	28 October	Wellington III	Pilot	Mine-laying off Stavanger. Weather bad. Land at Lossiemouth	5.20
42	9 November	Wellington III	Pilot	Operations on Hamburg. Weather bad	6.30
43	19 November	Wellington III	Pilot	Mine-laying off Saint-Nazaire. Successful. Land at St Eval	5.00

	Date	Aircraft	Position	Entry in logbook	flight time
44	22 November	Wellington III	Pilot	Operations on Stuttgart. Successful. Land at Oakington	6.50
45	18 December	Wellington III	Pilot	Portreath–Gibraltar	5.50
46	29 December	Wellington III	Pilot	Operations on Bizerta. Successful	5.10
	1943				
47	3 January	Wellington III	Pilot	Operations on Bizerta. Successful	5.50
48	7 January	Wellington III	Pilot	Operations on Bizerta. Successful	5.30
49	10 January	Wellington III	Pilot	Operations on Bizerta. Target located	5.35
50	16 January	Wellington III	Pilot	Operations on Bizerta. Successful	5.10
51	20 January	Wellington III	Pilot	Operations on Bizerta. Successful	4.55
52	23 January	Wellington III	Pilot	Operations on Bizerta. Successful	4.50
53	30 January	Wellington III	Pilot	Operations on Bizerta. Successful	5.05
54	1 February	Wellington III	Pilot	Operations on Trapani. Successful	6.10
55	7 February	Wellington III	Pilot	Operations on Villacidro. Successful	5.10
56	13 February	Wellington III	Pilot	Operations on Bizerta. Successful	5.30
57	23 February	Wellington III	Pilot	Operations on Bizerta. Successful	5.10
58	3 March	Wellington III	Pilot	Operations on Tunis. Successful	6.00
59	12 March	Wellington III	Pilot	Operations on Tunis. Successful	5.35
60	20 March	Wellington III	Pilot	Operations on Ferryville. Successful	5.15
61	21 March	Wellington III	Pilot	Operations on El Maou, Sfax. Successful	5.40
62	1 April	Wellington III	Pilot	Operations on Bizerta. Target located	5.20

Target map 'Airport' Brussels (Evere)
Richard Pinkham's first operational target, 2 July 1940.

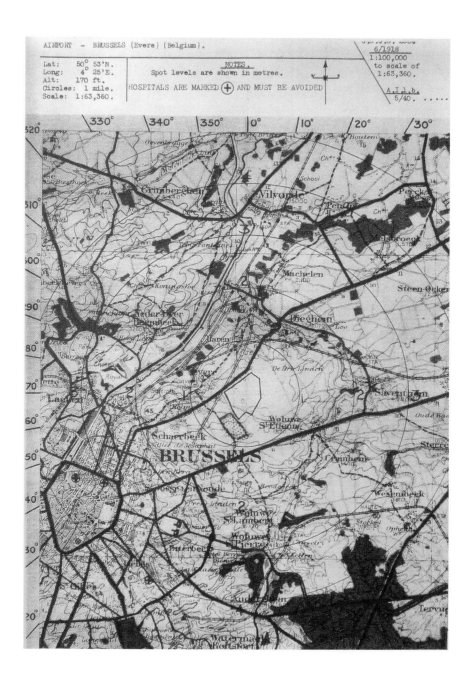

Appendix 3

Wing Commander Richard Pinkham DFC, Statistical Analysis of Chances of Survival in Operations over Germany

Richard Pinkham was credited with carrying out forty-four operational sorties against the enemy while flying from the UK. The table below demonstrates that Richard had about a 1 in 5 (22/100) chance of survival.

	Date	Target	Bomber Command sorties	Losses	Loss rate (%)	Cumulative attrition
1	2 July 1940	Evere–Brussels	66	0	0.0	100
2	19 July 1940	Bremen	89	3	3.4	97
3	21 July 1940	Kassel	81	1	1.2	95
4	9 August 1940	Mannheim	38	0	0.0	95
5	12 August 1940	Heringen	79	5	6.3	89
6	14 August 1940	Bordeaux	92	4	4.3	86
7	18 August 1940	Milan	24	0	0.0	86
8	2 September 1940	Frankfurt	84	3	3.6	82
9	8 September 1940	Ostend	133	8	6.0	77
10	10 September 1940	Search – N.Sea	n.a.	n.a.	n.a.	n.a.
11	13 September 1940	Calais	92	2	2.2	76
12	15 September 1940	Ostend	155	0	0.0	76
13	22 September 1940	Dresden	104	0	0.0	76
14	2 October 1940	Rotterdam	81	2	2.5	74
15	7 October 1940	Amsterdam	140	1	0.7	73
16	20 October 1940	Weseling	139	4	2.9	71
17	26 October 1940	Pölitz	89	0	0.0	71
18	29 October 1940	Magdeburg	104	1	1.0	71

Date		Target	Bomber Command sorties	Losses	Loss rate (%)	Cumulative attrition
19	5 January 1940	Turin	105	4	3.8	68
20	10 November 1940	Dresden	114	2	1.8	67
21	12 November 1940	Weseling	77	1	1.3	66
22	14 November 1940	Berlin	85	10	11.8	58
23	16 November 1940	Hamburg	145	3	2.1	57
24	3 December 1940	Mannheim	20	1	5.0	54
25	10 December 1940	Mannheim	67	3	4.5	52
26	15 December 1940	Magdeburg	79	3	3.8	50
27	21 December 1940	Merseburg	77	0	0.0	50
28	27 December 1940	Bordeaux	75	2	2.7	48
29	2 January 1941	Bremen	141	0	0.0	48
30	10 February 1941	Hanover	222	4	1.8	47
31	31 July 1942	Düsseldorf	630	29	4.6	45
32	28 August 1942	Saarbrücken	113	7	6.2	42
33	8 September 1942	Frankfurt	249	7	2.8	41
34	10 September 1942	Düsseldorf	479	33	6.9	38
35	14 September 1942	Bremen	446	21	4.7	37
36	16 September 1942	Essen	369	39	10.6	33
37	18 September 1942	Lorient	115	5	4.3	31
38	19 September 1942	Saarbrücken	118	5	4.2	30
39	10 December 1942	Saint-Nazaire	47	0	0.0	30
40	22 October 1942	Ruhr	22	0	0.0	30
41	28 October 1942	Stavanger	9	1	11.1	27
42	9 November 1942	Hamburg	213	15	7.0	25
43	19 November 1942	Saint-Nazaire	11	1	9.1	23
44	22 November 1942	Stuttgart	222	10	4.5	22
	Total		**5,840**	**240**	**4.1**	

Notes

1 For operations 1–29 the 'sorties' and 'Losses' figures refer to the total number of sorties to all targets on that night

2 For operations 30–44 the 'sorties' and 'Losses' figures are for each specific raid

3 The 'Losses' figure is for aircraft lost over enemy territory and does not include crashes in England or aircraft shot down by enemy intruders.

4 The 'Cumulative attrition' is indicative of the cumulative effect of the loss rate, with a starting point of 100 aircraft

5 The loss statistics are drawn from Martin Middlebrook and Chris Everitt, *The Bomber Command War Diaries: An Operational Reference Book, 1939–1945* (Midland Publishing, 1996).

Appendix 4

From Richard Pinkham, 'Introduction', *Accidents Information Bulletin,* **Issue 1, HQ RAF Burma**

Little progress seems to have been made in the reduction of flying accidents in the last six months [July to December 1944]. This can be best brought home to everybody when you see the outstanding figure of 416 aircraft damaged or destroyed by accidents in RAF Bengal/Burma in six months, *without one shot being fired by the enemy*. The number of aircraft lost due to enemy action represents but a small portion of the total losses of aircraft. Pilots, in whose hands the solution principally lies, must realise the seriousness of this implication; so many accidents are completely avoidable, and most of them are easily avoided. Give it a thought for a moment and you will realise the enormous wastage involved. Figures cannot give a sufficiently impressive picture of the situation. Each individual pilot must stop and realise how much these accidents affect the course of the war.

Four hundred aircraft out of action takes a lot of understanding. Try and imagine these four hundred aircraft on one mission; think how useful a force of that size would be in this theatre. All these accidents are aircraft which have been immobilised for a period of forty-eight hours or more, and in many cases the aircraft is completely lost as well as the crew. We can ill afford to waste such valuable material and life. The responsibility lies heavily on the shoulders of all those concerned, but if you wish to see this war won quickly, then a considerably greater effort must be made on the part of all concerned to reduce this appallingly high number of accidents.

Some readers of this Bulletin may feel that their unit's accident rate is after all not so bad, but until all preventable accidents are avoided no exertions can be too great to save the lives, the aircraft and the manpower which are now being needlessly wasted.

Richard Pinkham W/C
For Air Marshal, Commanding
RAF Bengal/Burma
March 1945

Appendix 5

**Details of the principal Bomber Command aircraft types
flown by Richard Pinkham.** (Source – Jonathan Falconer's *Bomber
Command Handbook 1939 – 1945* (Sutton Publishing, 2003)).

Armstrong-Whitworth Whitley

Type: twin-engined five-man mid-wing heavy night bomber.

Powerplant: Mk I, two 795hp Armstrong Siddeley Tiger IX
14-cylinder air-cooled radial engines; Mk II and III,
845hp Tiger VIII; Mk IV, two Rolls-Royce Merlin IV
12-cylinder liquid-cooled two-stage supercharged in-line
engines; Mk V, 1,145hp Merlin X.

Dimensions: span 84ft 0in, length 69ft 3in (Mk V 70ft 6in),
height 15ft 0in, wing area 1,137 sq ft.

Weights: Mk II and III, empty 15,475lb, loaded 22,900lb; Mk V,
empty 19,350lb, loaded 33,500lb.

Performance: Mk II and III, max speed 209mph at 16,400ft, service
ceiling 23,000ft, range 1,315 miles. Mk V, max speed
230mph at 16,400ft, service ceiling 26,000ft, range
1,500 miles.

Armament: Defensive: 1 x .303in Browning mg in Nash and
Thompson nose turret, 4 x .303in Browning mgs in
Nash and Thompson tail turret. Offensive: max bomb
load 7,000lb.

Production: 1,811 (excl. Prototypes).

Vickers-Armstrong Wellington

Type: twin-engined five-man mid-wing monoplane medium
                night bomber.
Powerplant: Mk I, two 1,000hp Bristol Pegasus X and XVIII
                air-cooled radial engines. Mk II, 1,145hp Rolls-Royce
                Merlin X in-line liquid-cooled in-line engines. Mk III,
                1,500hp Bristol Hercules XI sleeve-valve radials.
                Mk X, 1,675hp Bristol Hercules VI/XVI radials.
Dimensions: span 86ft 2in, length 64ft 7in, height 17ft 5in,
                wing area 840 sq ft.
Weights: Mk Ic, empty 18,556lb, loaded 28,500lb. Mk X,
                empty 22,474lb, loaded 36,500lb.
Performance: Mk Ic, max speed 235mph at 15,500ft, service ceiling
                18,000ft. Mk III, max speed 255mph at 12,500ft, service
                ceiling 18,000ft. Range with 4,500lb bomb load
                1,540 miles.
Armament: Defensive: Mk Ic, 2 x .303in Browning mgs in Frazer-
                Nash nose and tail turrets, 2 x manually operated
                Browning .303in mgs in beam positions. Offensive: max
                bomb load 4,500lb.
                Mk III, defensive: 2 x Browning .303in mgs in Frazer-
                Nash nose turret, four in Frazer-Nash rear turret,
                2 x manually operated Browning .303in mgs in beam
                positions. Offensive: max bomb load 4,500lb.
Production: 11,460.

Notes

Chapter 2: War and Reality

1. M. Middlebrook and C. Everitt, *The Bomber Command War Diaries: An Operational Reference Book, 1939–1945* (Midland Publishing, 1996).

2. W. R. Chorley, *Royal Air Force Bomber Command Losses of the Second World War Volume 1: Aircraft and Crews Lost during 1939–1940* (Midland Publishing, 1992).

3. The No. 77 Squadron ORB has the Whitley V of Pilot Officer North detailed to attack Kassel aircraft factory that night. The 'Details of Sortie of flight' section notes: 'P/O North attacked the target from 7,000 feet. The first stick of bombs was not observed. The second stick hit the target, but no fires as a result were seen. An intense AA barrage was encountered and many searchlights.' Other aircraft from the squadron that night attacked secondary targets, and one mentions seeing a fire near Bremen. Richard's recollection of the night is based upon his diary, and, in this author's experience (Steve Darlow), squadron diaries are not always accurate. As such it is most likely that Richard is recalling an attack on Bremen.

4. Chorley, *RAF Bomber Command Losses of the Second World War Volume 1*.

5. There is a slight discrepancy here with the No. 77 Squadron ORB, which states: 'P/O Brownlie was caught in a concentration of searchlights, and was forced to jettison his bombs, and then pretend to be disabled in order to throw off the searchlights. Even then it took him twenty to thirty minutes to get clear.'

6. Chorley, *RAF Bomber Command Losses of the Second World War Volume 1*.

7. Chorley, *RAF Bomber Command Losses of the Second World War Volume 1*.

Chapter 4: Not Likely to Forget

1. There is an inconsistency here between Richard's account and the

squadron records. The No. 77 Squadron ORB records that 'P/O Pinkham returned with bombs which failed to release due to accumulator being disconnected'. Richard's recollection of the raid is quite clear and is based upon notes written at the time.

2. Quotations and statistics from W. Shirer, *The Rise and Fall of the Third Reich* (Secker and Warburg Ltd, 1991).

Chapter 5: A Respite – of Sorts

1. W. R. Chorley, *Royal Air Force Bomber Command Losses Volume 7: Operational Training Units 1940–1947* (Midland Publishing, 2002).

2. Although this was deemed a 1,000-bomber raid, the actual number despatched fell just short of the four-figure mark at 956.

Chapter 6: Once More unto the Breach

1. Sir Charles Webster and Noble Frankland, *The Strategic Air Offensive against Germany, 1939–1945* (HMSO, 1961), pp. 135–6.

2. Webster and Noble, *The Strategic Air Offensive against Germany, 1939–1945*, p. 144.

3. W. R. Chorley, *Royal Air Force Bomber Command Losses of the Second World War Volume 3: Aircraft and Crew Losses 1942* (Midland Publishing, 1994).

4. Chorley, *RAF Bomber Command Losses of the Second World War Volume 3*.

Chapter 8: Preparing the Airmen

1. Chorley, *RAF Bomber Command Losses of the Second World War Volume 7*.

Sources

Primary Sources
The vast majority of this book is based upon notes kept by Richard
Pinkham, along with his logbook. The Operations Record Books of
No. 77 Squadron, No. 150 Squadron, No. 10 OTU and No. 82 OTU
have provided the official background to Richard's wartime flying
career. These are held at The National Archives in Kew, London, and
have the following file references:
TNA: PRO AIR 27/655: No. 77 Squadron ORB
TNA: PRO AIR 27/1010 and AIR 27/1011: No. 150 Squadron ORB
TNA: PRO AIR 29/638: No. 10 OTU ORB
TNA: PRO AIR 29/687: No. 82 OTU

With respect to Richard's time in Burma the following official
documents were referred to:
TNA: PRO AIR 41/36: Air Historical Branch: Narratives and
Monographs: The Campaigns in the Far East, Vol. III: India
Command.
TNA: PRO AIR 41/37: Air Historical Branch: Narratives and
Monographs: The Campaigns in the Far East, Vol. V: Air Supply
Operations in Burma, 1942–1945.
TNA: PRO AIR 23/2129: Burma Air Victory Dec. 1943–June 1945
(Eastern Air Command magazine).

Secondary Sources
W. R. Chorley's excellent *RAF Bomber Command Losses* series (Midland
Publishing) has enabled us to provide further detail to the losses
suffered by No. 77 Squadron, No. 150 Squadron and the Operational
Training Units with which Richard served. Martin Middlebrook and
Chris Everitt's essential Bomber Command research tool, *The Bomber*

Command War Diaries: An Operational Reference Book, 1939–1945 (Midland Publishing, 1996), has provided the context for many of the raids that Richard fought through. Jonathan Falconer's *Bomber Command Handbook, 1939–1945* (Sutton Publishing, 1999) filled in the technical gaps in our knowledge of the bomber war.

Index